22
H

Grace Episcopal Church
419 S. Main St.
Lexington, N.C. 27292

Aging, Death, Grief

D0856525

PARTNERS IN LOVE

INGREDIENTS FOR A DEEP AND LIVELY MARRIAGE

PARTNERS IN LOVE

INGREDIENTS FOR A DEEP AND LIVELY MARRIAGE

Alanson B. Houghton

Walker and Company
New York

First published in the United States of America
in 1988 by the Walker Publishing Company, Inc.

Published simultaneously in Canada by Thomas Allen & Son
Canada, Limited, Markham, Ontario.

Library of Congress Cataloging-in-Publication Data

Houghton, Alanson B.
    Partners in love.

    Includes index.
    1. Marriage—United States. 2. Marriage—
Religious aspects—Episcopal Church. I. Title.
HQ734.H865   1988   306.8'1   87-29486
ISBN 0-8027-1005-0

Printed in the United States of America

10 9 8 7 6 5 4 3 2 1

For Billie—for my children and hers—*and* for all those who by allowing me into their private corners opened my eyes, my heart, and my mind.

Special thanks to the Walkers, who were willing to publish this book; to Patricia Chao and Susan Gies, who patiently and gracefully edited it; and Pat Brigman and Kim Uhnavy, who coped with my writing and typed the manuscript twice!

CONTENTS

PREFACE

*Marriage is a life where each asks from
each what each most wants to give—and
each awakes in each what else would never
be.*

—EDWIN MUIR,
quoted by the Archbishop of Canter-
bury at the marriage of Prince
Charles and Lady Diana

*T*his is a relatively short and
simple book on an extraordinarily long and complex subject.
It comes largely out of my own experience as someone who
has been through most of the chairs of life.

I am an Episcopal minister who has been divorced and
remarried. My wife and I have nine children and seven grandchildren between us. I was the rector of parishes in Cleveland
and New York, where the focus of my pastoral ministry
centered on marriage counseling. My fifteen years in the glass
business before that, coupled with an M.B.A. from Harvard,
helped me develop a pragmatism about marriage that is re-

flected in these pages. My wife is a marriage and family therapist, which has also broadened my horizons, and it is out of this mélange that this "road map" for marriages emerges.

Against the advice of some I wrote this book for me. I wrote it because I wish that I could have given such a guide to couples preparing for marriage and couples adjusting to its wonders and its wobbles. I wrote it because this is what I think it takes to be PARTNERS IN LOVE in the deepest and broadest sense of those words. Finally, I wrote it because I am convinced that a deep and lively marriage needs tuning on a regular basis *and* needs to be held up and measured against real life—not fantasy or fiction!

The couples I admire and respect the most are those who take each other seriously enough to openly and courageously deal with their inevitable differences, and who love each other enough to do this without losing the essential glue and commitment that undergird their relationship.

INTRODUCTION

Marriages are made, not in heaven, but by wonderfully fallible human beings who hope for the best, but who often do precious little to make this most challenging and complicated relationship work. We fall in love and into marriage but that is just the beginning.

My first marriage failed because it never really went beyond that. I was ill prepared, sought no help, and led my life in isolation. I live with the knowledge that I was at least fifty percent responsible for its demise. My second marriage is great, but I am a different person in a different place. Getting help is as important to me as telling others to get it—in other words, I now practice what I preach! My wife and I thoroughly enjoy each other, we work together on our life, and we are jointly responsible for the marriage. We are partners—partners in love—in deed as well as word.

Marriage partners and their partnerships are the foci of this book. We normally think of partnerships in more commercial terms such as lawyers or co-owners of a business. It is easy to see what makes these work or causes them to fail. We can point to the ingredients that seem to make them click: choice of partners, trust, commitment, good judgment, willingness to take risks, speaking up, listening, asking for help, clear priorities and expectations, respect, humor, hard work, and last and maybe the most important of all—the capacity to deal with and resolve conflict!

Why can't we translate what proves so successful in the professional part of our lives into our private realm as well? Why not marriage partnerships? Why not a partnership of love into which we are willing to invest as much of ourselves as we do to become professionally and financially successful? What keeps us from investing the same knowledge, imagination, energy, caring, and time in that potentially remarkable partnership out of which comes our children and within which life and love can be experienced at their fullest?

This book is divided into two sections—the first dealing with foundations of a marriage partnership. These are the required building blocks necessary to keeping a structure erect and safe. The same is true of marriage. As you look down the Table of Contents you will recognize familiar concepts, words, ideas that are applicable to all marriages. They are the basics to a life lived in partnership with another human being. For instance, we all choose and are chosen; we all have feelings whether we deal with them or not; we all change as the years move on.

The second part of the book looks at the private sides of our marriage partnerships—those individual and quiet and complicated aspects of our experiences and personalities that we bring to the relationship. Here we learn from the experience that grows out of our own emerging needs, and we learn from our partners as we become more sensitive to what they want and need as well.

What is within these covers is what I would discuss with you if we were sitting face to face in my office. In my twenty-plus years as a priest/counselor I have found that each of these areas needs to be looked at and dealt with in depth—before *and* during a marriage. Marriage partnerships require a lot of work and homework. Maybe this book will serve as a checklist, a guide, a reminder, an impetus to get help "early and often."

Good luck and Godspeed as you learn and love and live out your lives together in that extraordinary and special partnership known as marriage.

THE FOUR INGREDIENTS OF A DEEP AND LIVELY MARRIAGE

A deep and lively love! That is what it's all about. That is the image, the dream, the hope we all have as we exchange our marriage vows.

That's the good news. The more difficult news is that you and your partner are very different people. You must learn to see yourself and others as: 1) individual, independent, unique persons and as 2) members of a unit, a team, a partnership.

Your spouse is not a mirror image of you or of anyone else! Yet we all share the same four basic sides to our natures. It is your acceptance and understanding that we are all 1) physical, 2) thinking, 3) emotional, and 4) spiritual begins that can broaden, deepen, and enrich your marriage partnership. Look hard at yourself and your partner as you see these four ingredients in both of you in quite different but quite fascinating ways. Allow yourself to be what you are and how you were created!

ALLOW YOURSELF TO BE A PHYSICAL BEING

Just as we all feel both pain and pleasure within our bodies and we all abhor pain, most of us like to be held, hugged, stroked, and kissed. Our sexuality is such an integral and important part of our psychological and physiological expression and enjoyment that to deny ourselves such God-given pleasure is sinful.

Your partner can awaken in you such incredible desire and joy and fulfillment, if you will let them, and if you are caring and careful in return.

Age is really no barrier to sexual pleasure. Responses do tend to slow down as bodies do, but intercourse can be just as wonderful at three score and ten years as it was at twenty-one.

Even more than sex itself is the physical connections you

make with the one you love—the touch of a hand, the feel of a pat, the sense of their physical presence close at hand. Our bodies are the most visible *us*, the most tactile side of our being, the initial presenter of who we are. You should rejoice in your good fortune, rather than try to hide or subjugate what you have been given to live within and enjoy throughout your life on earth. Pleasure, not pain, is God's wish for us all.

ALLOW YOURSELF TO BE A THINKING BEING

You have an enormous capacity for learning to do all sorts of things and about all sorts of things. Closed minds at any age can close down a marriage partnership, destroy a relationship, and literally stunt your growth. It is amazing how the more information you absorb, the more tolerant you become; the more you know, the better you can cope. Partners who expand their base of knowledge together may well not agree on everything, but in the end, they will end up closer. Newspapers, books, current events, the theater, politics, the arenas for learning and discussion are countless, but you have to be willing to open your mind to new currents and be willing to change if convinced otherwise. Couples who have the capacity to talk, argue, agree, and disagree on issues that frame their wider life are indeed fortunate, for therein lies the real world in which they must live and work and contribute. Partners who know that each one is well informed can experience the joy of growing together intellectually. Knowledge can only broaden and deepen healthy partnerships.

ALLOW YOURSELF TO BE AN EMOTIONAL BEING

You have deep feelings that profoundly affect your intimate relationships. While there are no right or wrong feelings, there are right or wrong ways of expressing them and handling them. There may be no "good time" to let feelings out, but timing can help set the stage and cause the news to be less threatening to the listener. The listener has the more complicated task of listening without rebuttal or rejection of the speaker. If you *love* each other enough to *trust* each other enough you will be able to strip naked emotionally without fear of shame or judgment. You respect both your partner and the intimacy required to maintain such a unique relationship.

When a bee stings, you say "ouch." When a cat nuzzles, you purr. Why should your human experiences be more bottled up? Emotions are the matrix of your experience and of your expectations. They cannot always be matched, but they can be looked at calmly and caringly for clues that will help you better love and understand your partner for life.

ALLOW YOURSELF TO BE A SPIRITUAL BEING

This fourth aspect tends to get either too little notice or too much focus. We are all searching for all sorts of things in all sorts of ways. We peer over walls or around corners or out windows. We peer into books and into each other's eyes, into history and into the Bible. We are forever asking the ultimate questions—What? Why? Where? and How? *We search for God.*

If you can admit this need for clarity and for answers, and explore the spiritual searching side of life together as a new adventure, your lives together as husband and wife, as parents and as people, will be incredibly enriched. It ties everything else together. It also ties you closer to the Eternal, which then permits you to lead your lives with more purpose, less worry, and with certain hope.

As in anything else, balance is crucial. God works through you. *You* are responsible for your words and your deeds. Spirituality should not be confused with a narrow, pietistic self-serving view of God that tries to make him into a fixer rather than a savior; an excuse for avoiding life rather than the reason for plunging in.

THE FOUNDATIONS OF A MARRIAGE PARTNERSHIP

ROMANCE
AND
REALITY

Tradition wears a snowy beard
Romance is always young
—JOHN GREENLEAF WHITTIER
("Mary Garvin," Stanza 4)

*I*t's fun sometimes, isn't it, to go to the movies and watch an entire courtship and marriage begin, continue, and flourish in ninety minutes or less? That's romance, you think to yourself. When you come out of the theater and plunge back home into the routine of your daily life, you get a sure, swift kick back into reality. While you might feel a momentary twinge of remorse ("Why can't life really be like that?"), something inside you knows that in the real world all is not wine and roses forever.

You fall head over heels in love with another human being who is obviously the most beautiful, handsome, amusing, smart, sensitive, and sane individual you have ever met. Then over a period of time you find that the person has "warts." He doesn't like your mother, or her political opinions seem some-what outrageous, or he doesn't respond with the identical passionate feelings you happen to have at particular times. That is the difference between romance and reality! My own wife claims that one of the things that first attracted her to me was my impulsiveness, yet it is that same trait, once we were married, that became not only less appealing but threatening.

A balance of both romance *and* reality is crucial to any relationship that is to deepen, grow and flourish. However, each needs to be looked at separately and as opposite sides of the same person. This is where people often get confused and discouraged. It seems incomprehensible that a perfect lover would act in imperfect ways. Yet that is exactly what happens. What makes someone the perfect lover in your mind is that you have idealized him or her. But that is not the *real* person! The real person must sooner or later emerge, and it is not the end of the world when they do. In fact, it may well be the beginning of a fabulous relationship. You gain rather than lose something, and what you gain is a real, live three-dimensional human being instead of a one-dimensional image.

ROMANCE IS ALWAYS YOUNG

As John Greenleaf Whittier wrote, "Romance is always young." What a wonderful metaphor! Romance is always young, fresh, fascinating, uncluttered, totally absorbing, and uncomplicated by whatever else is going on around or within you. Romance is a fabulous and exciting and important rite of passage. It can unleash your finest instincts and surface your most thoughtful impulses. You are never more attuned, attentive, or attractive. Romance focuses your entire attention on another human being. That in itself is good, for it forces you—maybe for the first time—to look seriously at someone other than yourself.

Romance also energizes you as nothing else can. You are "turned on." You make wild statements, do silly things, use terrible judgment. You go after the object of your affection with a determination and energy that could move mountains. You must have that other person for your own. Songs, stories, poetry, a certain smell or garment or look can turn you into an incoherent, wily beast who is determined to corner and capture its prey! No one can talk you out of it, for, like fever, it has to run its course. My father once remarked that trying to talk sense to someone in love was like trying to convince a dog in heat to stay in its own yard.

When doing premarital counseling, I found that people in love feel more than they listen; they glow more than they think. They really don't want to look into the mirror of reality for very long periods of time. That seems to be both the wonder and the worry of romance, and that is also how Romeo and Juliet got into such deep trouble.

Romance is such an expected and integral part of the human courting/mating dance that you should relax and enjoy it while it runs its course. I am certainly not proposing that you lose sight of those wonderful "in love" feelings you have had for another. In fact, I suggest that you savor them. Take a moment to do the following exercise.

EXERCISE 1
Your Vision of Your Partner

1. Jot down those "in love" feelings you feel or once felt for your partner—images, your dreams, your aspirations, the promises you made.
2. Spend a moment or two reflecting about each one.
3. What has changed—for better or worse.

Whether you are looking forward to a marriage or back at a marriage use the above exercise to write down what you feel or once felt about that other person. That list represents "a vision" of the person. It may be only part of the story, but it is a snapshot of the real human being to whom you are so connected.

A wonderful cartoon appeared in *The New Yorker*, which will warm any romantic heart, *but* makes a tough point as well. It shows a past-middle-age man turning to his past-middle-age wife, sitting beside him on a bench, and saying, "I must be nuts, but after forty-eight years, I'm still gaga about you." On one level that's a neat, romantic image, and it is how I want to feel about my wife after forty-eight years. But on another level—if you stop and think a minute—it pictures a couple who have lived with each other and survived together for forty-eight years. That can only mean one thing. They have dealt with the *reality* of their love, their lives, their marriage, and themselves!

THE REALITY FACTOR

Reality has to be factored into "love"—into your relationship, into your marriage. Otherwise, it is doomed to failure or a living death. The other side of the person you want to marry or did marry happens to be a real human being, which inevitably means a *less romantic* one!

So blinded by passion, we all tend to forget we have fallen in love with an idealized image who has been put on a pedestal. You have also fallen in love with a partial reflection of yourself, which is very narcissistic. What happens when the real person emerges? How do you feel about him now that he has stepped off the pedestal? Can you accept him as an imperfect human being, yet realize he still has what attracted you to him in the first place? Can you deal with his humanity as the glitter wears off and the pulls of daily living crowd in and distract?

The answer is *Yes*, but you must incorporate reality into your romantic vision. A friend's in-law once remarked, "When I stopped hearing bells, the marriage stopped." It sounds like he was unable and probably unwilling to see reality injected into his marriage. He wanted the honeymoon to last forever. But romance with no reality equals a dead marriage.

I'm reminded of a couple I once worked with. They were having a whirlwind courtship and were seriously talking about marriage. Both had come out of other marriages without adequately dealing with their pasts. They were deeply attracted to each other physically and I think emotionally, but they got caught up in the logistics of who would live where, when, and how. They never gave themselves a chance to develop any romantic rhythm or fun or time together, much less deal with the realities of children, money, age difference, hang-ups, and expectations. They came to see me because they were mad at each other.

No wonder. I advised them to not even think about getting married for six months, to go back to square one and simply enjoy each other; to play, court, talk, love, or whatever; then see where they were and come back to deal with some of the realities. They never came back, nor did they continue the relationship! They were romantics, not realists. They either couldn't accept or weren't attracted enough to the real person.

The other side of the equation was a couple who were crazy about each other but whose professional and personal commitments made it impossible for them to marry for at least two years. It *was* tough, but their romantic love, coupled with their "real" love gave them the strength to focus on what was ultimately important.

Romance is fun, but reality *must* be there as well. I cannot emphasize this enough! You have to love another person as another person, not just as an ideal or a reflection of yourself. You must be able to see how that difference can be enhancing, not threatening.

Infatuation is not love, and how you spot the difference is how well you learn "to love" the real person you are so much "in love with." When we first fall in love, we tend to have a hard time staying out of bed! However, when we've really loved and learned and lived with that person for a period of time we spend less time in bed but our sex life is usually a lot more satisfying. The passion has deepened. Our love has matured and our entire relationship, sexual and other aspects, is much broader and deeper.

SEEING BOTH SIDES

Flip Wilson used to say on TV, "What you sees is what you gets," and you do need to see both sides of the same human being—the romantic and the real—*and* to try to accept and love them both! Take a look at the following examples of romance and reality in operation—two ways of looking at qualities of the same person.

Romance	*Reality*
She's beautiful!	She's beautiful *and* very bright! Is she brighter than I am?
He's so thoughtful	He cares for everyone and I mean everyone! Does this mean I'll be just one of the crowd?
She is very competent.	She is a real professional. In fact, her earnings are approaching mine!
He is so overpowering! I feel cared for and protected.	He makes me feel a little fenced in. I don't want to be "owned" by anyone.
She is very sexy.	Other men are always gawking at her. I'm proud of her, but I'm jealous.
He's a real man.	He's too macho sometimes. He never tells me how he feels. I've never seen him cry.
The children just love her.	The children are beginning to have problems with my new wife.

He is a fabulous lover.	He always wants to make love. Can't he realize that quality, not quantity, is the best measure?
She is so well informed and always stands up for what she believes in.	I wish she'd stuck with the facts before she'd said that. I know we don't have to think alike but . . .
He has enough money so we shouldn't have any financial worries.	Why is he so tight at times? Isn't it *our* money?
She has a neat family.	I like her family, but they all talk on the phone all the time. I feel left out.
He takes charge.	I feel controlled. What I feel and want is important, isn't it?

In each of these cases, the person is the same. It is just that reality has tempered the romantic vision. The perception and the balances have shifted. The suitor has become the spouse. Where the romantic feelings were purely reactive, the reality experiences were much more reflective; same person—different perceptions. That is real life. That is the conflict between the ideal and the actual, the perfect and the flawed, the person you adore and the person you have to live with. If you can deal with these dichotomies and differences with patience, wisdom, understanding, and love, you stand a good chance of building a remarkable partnership. Rejoice in and don't be threatened by these natural differences.

A BRIDGE TOO FAR

Sometimes the romantic notion is so far removed from reality that bridging it is almost impossible. For instance, what about the person from a comfortable financial and educational background who falls in love with an uneducated, struggling, impoverished artist who assumes that details such as rent, food, and clothing will somehow take care of themselves? They usually don't and, although mundane in nature, those concerns can literally blow up a relationship.

What about the fifty-year-old boss who falls in love with his twenty-five-year-old secretary and divorces his wife in order to marry her? The movies make scenes like this turn out fine, but it rarely happens in real life. Rationales such as "I've never met a man like him before" or "She's the first person who has really understood me" just don't wash. The setting in which the romance was kindled is unreal, and the life these two would have together, in totally new roles, will probably be unreal as well.

Between these extremes are the couples who know better, but who get caught up in the realities before they have even talked about and translated their romantic feelings into more realistic expectations. One couple I worked with for six months almost ended their relationship two months before the planned wedding date. Much to their surprise, and mine, their expectations of each other had never really been heard or worked out. They had also moved into her new house, which made him feel uncomfortable, and he went on an extended business trip, which made her feel inadequate. The romance flew out the window. What they were eventually able to do was back off (they physically separated for a few weeks), talk, listen, renegotiate, "court," and then begin over again.

THE BEST AND THE BEAST

Love and marriage bring out the best and the beast in everyone. You need to admit that and work at bridging the gap between romance and reality. If you can do that early on and often, the odds are in your favor. How do you do it? Here is an exercise that should help.

EXERCISE 2
Reality Checking

1. Find that list on which you wrote your romantic feelings for your partner (see Exercise 1). Turn the paper over and write down some of the realities that you now see in the real person who has emerged out of the mist of love! One piece of paper with writing on both sides equals one person with two sides. Both sides and both lists are valid, for they represent—together—the whole person, and you have to deal with that whole person. The romantic feelings are fine. They just need to be deepened and broadened with the facts.

2. Talk about these differences with your partner. It is fine to say "I love your body, but not every night," or "I'm threatened by your success," or "Your family bugs me," or whatever else is beginning to separate and alienate you from one another.

   The deeper your love, the more open you can be! If you are too fragile to deal with the truth, then you are too fragile to withstand an open and mature relationship.

Romance and reality represent dreams, facts, hopes, fears, promises, challenges, warm fuzzies, *and* warts! You must respect them both. You must recognize them for what they are. You must use them to enrich and deepen your marriage partnership. As *The New Yorker* cartoon suggested, it is wonderful to be gaga about your spouse, *but* be gaga about the real human being underneath that "vision" who first blinded you with love!

CHOICE
AND
COMMITMENT

True happiness consists not in the multitude
of friends, but in the worth and choice.

—BEN JONSON
("Cynthia's Revels," Act IV)

Choice is our privilege. Commitment is our promise. In marriage they go hand in hand, literally!

You are both a chooser and one who is chosen. The act of choosing is probably the most important decision you'll ever make, and to "be chosen" is the most important thing that will happen to you. Act on the first and receive the second with all the wisdom and humility at your disposal.

Commitment takes you into deeper water, for here you connect with and bind yourself to another for a long period of time. You'd better be very sure when you make a commitment, for to undo such a promise a month, a year, or many years hence will cause only turmoil and pain.

Ben Jonson warns about choice and its effect on "true happiness." Indeed the choice of a partner for any endeavor requires a lot of thought. You wouldn't ask someone who has never had a rifle in his hands to go deer hunting. You wouldn't go into business with a total stranger. Even blind dates get checked out beforehand. Multiply these and other examples a thousand times and you begin to see the magnitude and importance of the choice of your partner in marriage, *and* their choice of you as well.

A CHOICE FOR LIFE

The choice of a marriage partner is a choice for life! You who are about to formalize that choice and those of you who have lived with that choice for a period of time are not in such different places. Choices need to be made, remade, and reexamined over a lifetime.

You not only choose for life, choose another person to be your marriage partner, but in that choice countless others are involved as well. You choose families, friends, potential children.

Your choice must not only mirror your love for each other but it must accurately reflect the facts. It is also a choice that can be undone a lot easier before a marriage than afterward.

Above all, marriage is a choice—a free, informed, open, considered, and considerate "asking" of another human being to share your growing up and growing old, your hopes and fears, your dreams, your bed, your board, your thoughts, your idiosyncrasies, your journey through life. When you stop and think about the privilege *and* responsibility of "having and holding" another human being—a child of God—"from this day forward" (to quote from the Episcopal marriage service), it should make you a lot more conscious of how important your act of choosing is and how careful and clear that choice should be.

The younger you are, the more careless you are. As a friend of mine once quipped, "The only substitute for experience is to be seventeen years old." But there are older fools as well! You must be careful as you choose *and* whom you choose. You should choose in a partner what pleases you, but also what complements you; what broadens your horizons; what deepens your knowledge; what challenges you to be better than you are. That is tough to do when you are in love.

A COLD AND REALISTIC LOOK

For a moment let's look coldly and realistically at the person you are or were so enamored with. The following exercise will help.

EXERCISE 3
Looking and Thinking Hard

1. Try to visualize the person you love as your business or law partner.

2. Never mind his or her beauty, what about brains?
3. What about his or her temperament, staying power, humor, and the ability to change?
4. Never mind the kind words or the adoring looks, what would a supplier or a client or a customer see and hear?
5. Never mind that you have promised your future, your fortune, or whatever, just imagine that person twenty-five, forty, sixty years from now sitting in a rocking chair next to you.

You are not doing yourself or the other person a favor by failing to look at your choices and the reasons why you make them before signing a partnership agreement. In fact, it takes a rare degree of wisdom and caring to take one more look!

Before I was married in the early fifties, my fiancée broke the engagement a month before the wedding. I didn't ask why, nor did she tell me. That should have told us both something. What I did do was overwhelm her and talk her into marrying me. My choice was my ego rather than her feelings *or* the inherent problems we seemed destined to face. If she had been stronger or I had been wiser, we might have looked a lot harder at our choices before we got married.

WILL YOU HAVE THIS PERSON

"Will you have this person to be your husband or wife?" asks the marriage service. Translated literally, this asks if you choose this person to be your partner for life. Think about that, for life! Life can be "a sentence" or a joyful adventure, depending on how you have chosen. It is your free choice *and* it is your responsibility!

"To live together in the covenant of marriage" is the next reminder. Covenant means promise, and promises should not be lightly made. A promise is your word *and* your honor all wrapped up in one.

The question goes on, "Will you love, comfort, honor, and keep them in sickness and in health, forsaking all others, be faithful as long as you both shall live?" Your answer? "I will." Here we make the single most important choice we will ever make in our entire lives and yet we barely think about it! Why are we all so careless?

I think it's because we're scared to ask ourselves hard questions and to hear the answers. Ask yourself the questions in the following exercise.

EXERCISE 4
Tough Questions

1. Why do I, or did I, choose this person to be my partner for life?
2. Why do I think he/she chose me?
3. Would I choose to go into business with him/her? If so, why?
4. Do I feel I am or was chosen under pressure?
5. Am I or was I under pressure to make this choice?
6. Why should I *not* choose him/her to be my partner?
7. Why should he/she *not* choose me?

There are no right or wrong answers, but these questions— *all of them*—need to be answered before *and*/or after the fact. Choice is our privilege and a sound choice is our responsibility, particularly when it involves human lives and a lot of years. I have had couples decide the day before their wedding to call it off, and I can only tip my hat and applaud them for their candor and their courage. All the presents and plans and arrangements aren't worth a hoot, if there is a nagging uncertainty that we have made the wrong choice.

When I was in seminary, a classmate decided after three years of training that he did not want to be ordained. Initially, he had chosen not to go the final step, but his wife wouldn't hear of it and put enormous pressure on him. He was ordained. Years later I heard that he had been deposed and had left the ministry. What a waste. How weak of him and how insensitive of her.

Choice is your option alone and you'd better exercise it well for you have to live with its object. The choice of a marriage partner is one of the most exciting decisions you will ever make. The rechoosing of your spouse in different ways over the years is also exciting and enriching. Every day I rechoose my wife by my actions, through my words and thoughts. It isn't dramatic but it is a conscious reaffirmation of my love for her, a conscious appreciation of her love for me, and a fresh determination to deepen that commitment that gives our partnership its fire and its staying power.

UNTIL DEATH DO US PART: COMMITMENT

In the Old Testament there is a brief statement by a daughter-in-law to her mother-in-law that eloquently talks about choice and commitment and serves as a bridge between them. I wanted this passage read at my marriage to my present wife, but the clergyman said it didn't have anything to do with marriage! I disagree. It has everything to do with free choice and the commitment such a choice entails. It is also lyrical and beautiful.

Ruth said to Naomi, "For whither thou goest, I will go and whither thou lodgest, I will lodge. Thy people shall be my people, and thy God, my God."

It seems so simple and so direct and so easy. Would that it was and could be lived that completely. Ruth, as you know, married Boaz and, therefore, didn't go with Naomi. This is how it should have turned out, and Naomi knew that. But Ruth meant what she said at the time! We mean what we say at the time! We'd swear on a stack of Bibles, and we do almost exactly that when we swear before our friends and families and God that we "take" this person to be our wife or husband, "until we are parted at death." That's not for overnight. *It's forever*, and that's a long, long time.

What do you commit, what do you sign on for in this marriage partnership that is meant to go on forever?

1. You commit yourself to another human being, which means you give away part of yourself to that person, who, in turn, gives part of himself or herself to you. You exchange the ultimate gift. An old friend once wrote, "When we marry, we double ourselves."
2. You commit yourselves to each other's well being. You commit yourself to caring about the other as much as you care about yourself. And that is a lot!
3. You commit yourself to work at the marriage, and I mean

just that—WORK: effort, time, understanding, forgiveness.

4. You commit yourself, "for better or for worse," which is far easier to say than to live out. You make a bargain for the good times, as well as the bad. In fact, the word commitment comes alive when times are bad. It is the backdrop and landmark against which your integrity is measured.

5. You commit "for richer and for poorer," which means that you share what you have, regardless of how much or how little. A couple I know was about to go under financially (they eventually did take Chapter 11), but they shared their doubts, as well as their debts, and worked through the pain and embarrassment of being flat broke. Their marriage was a lot better after they faced their common problem with an openness and frankness and a sense of being "in the mud" together.

6. You commit "in sickness and in health." This is probably the toughest, for you do get sick and do grow old and forgetful, and you are less pretty as the years march on.

7. Finally, and the most encompassing of all, is that you commit "to love and to cherish" another human being over the period of a lifetime. This is and should be a lifelong commitment, unless something causes it "to die."

Can you or will you make such a commitment? It is easier to do so before a marriage than it is to reconnect and recommit in a different and deeper way halfway down the road. In either case you need to ponder this extraordinary statement by a minister and teacher, Dr. Diogenese Allen, who had this to say in his book *Temptations* (Cowley Press, Cambridge, Mass. 1986):

The sheltered lives we lead encourage us to become thoughtless. We are encouraged to flit from moment to moment, activity to activity, possession to possession, person to person. The beauty to be found only through commitment is thus inaccessible to us. In fact, we are increasingly told today that commitment is not beautiful. It is said, for example, that lifelong commitment in marriage is an arbitrary holdover from a bygone religious age. Actually, whatever marriage may be, it is not arbitrary. Its foundations are in the depths of our own person; it is in that deep longing genuinely to know another person and truly to be known ourselves. To hedge on our commitment to another is really to hedge on how much we think they are worth.

It takes time to discover worth. Its full depths are not apparent from the start. We have to venture, to act with faith that there is more than we have seen so far. A genuine marriage is a pledge of faith that we love enough to go into the future, with the confidence that another person is worthy of our lifelong devotion. It is also the humble reception of another person's faith in our being worthy of his or her lifelong devotion.

Being worthy of another's lifelong devotion is a pledge received and a pledge given and it is also "a pledge of faith."

WILL YOU MAKE SUCH A COMMITMENT?

Let me ask the question again. Can you and will you make such a commitment? The answer to "Can you?" is yes. The answer to "Will you?—Will you keep the commitment you make, regardless of good times or bad, good health or bad?" makes you pause, for the answer determines our futures.

When the rings are placed on each other's fingers, in the Episcopal service, each says, "This ring is a symbol of my vow, and with all that I am and all that I have, I honor you in the name of God." What an incredible promise! If worked on, lived with, loved through, adjusted, and deepened, it can herald a partnership of two people that literally can change two lives and make one marriage.

It is also "commitment" that, if only parenthesized in your minds or used for your own ends, can be an excuse to do nothing about an intolerable relationship or even to hide behind, if you feel you have been maligned or forgotten. Marriages can wear down, get sick, and die. Marriages sometimes fall apart, as individuals fall away from each other for a lot of complicated reasons. We will look at some of these reasons and at ways to stem the tide or change direction before it is too late. But at this juncture, it needs to be said again that "commitment" is a two-way street, a living expression of "chosen" people. If that mix changes and the commitment is no longer, it serves no useful purpose to keep up a façade for purely selfish reasons.

We've all seen couples who are "still together," when we know by their actions as well as their words that they can't stand each other. We've heard people say things like, "We stay together because of the children." I wonder how much they really care for their children versus their own reputation and image. Children are the first to spot trouble and to suffer because of it, for it is invariably acted out in their presence. "Marriage is for life," "We made a commitment to each other," "I've devoted my life to this person," are also accurate statements of feeling. But the question is whether they mirror reality or feelings of panic when our marriages slide into deep trouble.

It is interesting to note *who* makes these statements when a marriage falls apart—the one who leaves or the one who has left. *No one likes to be left or rejected.* No one likes to admit failure. But being imperfect creatures, we do fail in big ways. It is harder, but better, to deal with the facts than it is to hide behind the form or the institution of marriage.

You choose and are chosen by others to walk together through life. You make a commitment to do everything in your power to make that journey a deep, joyful, and fulfilling experience. You promise to hang in there for better or worse. *But our commitment is to each other, not just to an ideal.* Your commitment must be enfleshed and ennobled and not used as a weapon for selfish and desperate ends. Commitment is both a fabulous and a frightening act and you should keep that dichotomy in mind as you make it, examine it, renew it, and relive it with your partner.

Walter Lippman once wrote, "In foreign relations, as in all other relations, a policy has been formed only when commitments and power have been brought into balance." I end this chapter on choice and commitment with that thought, because it is so applicable to marriage. Choice is your opportunity to involve another human being in your journey through life. Commitment is your formalizing and ensuring that relationship. Power is what you put into the enterprise, and its use, its energy, and its focus largely determine the balance, which then has a lot to do with the health and the longevity of the marriage itself.

PRIORITIES AND EXPECTATIONS

The difficulty in life is the choice.
—GEORGE MOORE,
(The Bending of the Bough)

What we want and what we need, what we *think* should be and what *will* be are questions that are ever on our minds. Dealing with the first requires some disciplined thought such as prioritizing our feelings. What and whom is important—and in which order? Those become our starting priorities as we negotiate them against what we expect of someone else and they of us!

Priorities and expectations are intertwined. They reflect our dreams and the realities of everyday life. The difficulty of life *is* the choice, but its corollary and its balance are the expectations that make such choices possible and plausible.

What are your priorities? Before you have a chance to

overthink the question, jot some of yours down. What are your priorities? What do you feel is important in your life and for your happiness?

Is it to be loved? To be financially secure? To have a family? To be a success? To live in San Francisco? To have a condo in Florida? To stay healthy? To be happily married? To be active in the community? Make sure the list reflects your needs more than your wants.

Take a look at your list. Priorities need to be articulated before *and* during the course of a marriage. Were they? When was the last time, if ever, you discussed them?

Priorities reflect what you feel is important now and your partner deserves that information. Unless your priorities are on the table, it is hard for your partner to take your measure or to have an inkling as to what your values are.

You need to look at your priorities, as a single person, as a married person, as an individual in a marital partnership, and as an ideal.

If you are single and responsible only for yourself, your priorities will naturally reflect a certain narcissism and insularity. Since, technically, you can do what you want, how you want, when you want, without regard for another's inputs or feelings, your priorities might well include such things as personal happiness, job achievement, good health, a nice place to live, and an active social life.

If you are married or about to be, these priorities need adjustment. Your partner's needs and feelings will impinge on what you can and will do. Many of the same priorities listed above may sound the same, but they will mean something quite different. "Personal happiness" will involve two, instead of one, and that change is a lot more encompassing than it sounds. To get something, you usually have to give up something. In this case unfettered and unfiltered personal opinions and options.

A promotion and a raise may mean more money is available for family support but also a loss of control over where you live. A friend of mine was offered an enormous increase in salary, if he and his wife would move from one coast to the other. He did, but she didn't. Eventually, he came home. They could have saved their marriage a lot of wear and tear if their priorities had been in concert from the start.

As individuals in a marriage partnership, you need to list your priorities, talk about them, reflect on them, readjust them, and then accept them. If your partner's priorities seem out of kilter, or yours seem less than reasonable to him or her, you had better take another look at what you are getting into. Here is an example from a married couple I knew well.

They each wrote down their top five priorities in descending order. Here is what they wrote:

Her Priorities	*His Priorities*
1. Him	1. His career
2. Their marriage and family	2. Financial independence
3. A house in the country	3. A nice apartment
4. Financial security	4. Children and family life
5. A good life	5. Their marriage

Their differences in priorities shocked me more than it did them. They seemed to have accepted the differences as being normal for the early years of a marriage—he emphasized the job, she the hearth. Where the imbalance did damage, as they began to realize, was that, although his job occupied a large part of his waking thought, time, and effort, it was "for them and for her" that he struggled so hard! He needed to get his life into better balance, to realize that seventy hours a week working left little or no time for his wife and the marriage, which he said (and I think he believed it) was the reason for the grind in the first place! She in turn needed to appreciate his efforts, *but* to set some limits on his time away from her. Otherwise, she would begin to build a separate life and act out her anger, which became more evident as we talked, in inappropriate and destructive ways. They needed to renegotiate and to each give up—rather than give in—a piece of their own territory.

MY IDEAL LIST

I believe individuals in marriage relationships need to put that first; that is, the partnership itself. *That is the ideal.* It means the one partner heads the other partner's list. She is first on his and he is first on hers. This may sound too romantic, but, after all, isn't a marriage the result of two individuals falling enough in love with each other to radically change their lives and the focus of their attention? The answer had better be yes!

Let me give two very specific examples. "My children come first," says a mother who has forgotten she is first a wife! Where did the children come from? They came out of the union of a man and a woman who deeply loved each other and wanted children as an expression of that love. If children come first, they may end up last. Their parents' relationship is the most important and it must come first. Only out of a strong and deep and loving partnership can come the nurturing and love necessary to bring the children up and prepare them for their own adult lives.

"I have to work these crazy hours to support my family." Maybe so, but maybe he needs to support his ego at the expense of his family? Maybe he's a workaholic? In any case, he isn't much use to his wife (and children) if he is never at home, or if he is so pooped when he is there that he really isn't there at all! Priorities, priorities, priorities. Who and what are important?

My ideal list of personal priorities would be:

1. Wife.
2. Our marriage and the quality of our lives.
3. Our families and our health.
4. My work and the quality of that experience.
5. Her work and how I can support that.
6. Where we live (location, design, and ambiance).
7. How we live (money, security, and the extras).

Before you snicker, recheck your own priorities! You can get another job, but finding another spouse is a very painful and often impossible task. Your children grow up and leave— leaving you holding the bag, rather than your spouse, *if* you have neglected each other during those intervening years. You can get rich. You can have three houses. You can own a plane. You can constantly be surrounded by a lot of sycophantic friends, but "not have time" for a deep and joyful relationship. You can control a corporation, but lose control over yourself. You do have a choice, for *you* set the priorities!

FIVE GREAT EXPECTATIONS

"I didn't know you felt that way!" "Why didn't you tell me you only wanted one child?" "You want to have sex every day. You must be crazy!" "The church is very important to me. You know that!" "I want to make a lot of money before I'm forty." "I never thought you expected THAT!"

Expectations, anticipations, hopes. It is hard to find the exact word to describe what you look forward to in your relationship with another human being in marriage. In business you are careful to lay out all the expectations before you enter into a contractual relationship or sign any papers. I strongly recommend prenuptial discussions on what each partner expects in and out of the marriage partnership. The clearer you are about what you need from the other person, and the clearer he or she is about what they need from you, the better the marriage over the long haul. It isn't that you will necessarily have the same expectations, but you do need to minimize surprises and maximize mutual awareness, caring, and honesty.

Here's an example from my own life: My wife and I now live in South Carolina and we love it. Our mutual expectation is that we will live out our lives in this marvelous city of Charleston. We have articulated this feeling to each other. But sometimes life can throw us a curve. If suddenly I got a tempting call to take a parish in another city or my wife decided it would be wise for her to reopen her practice in New York, we would deal with these new inputs, *but* against the backdrop of a common knowledge and similar expectations. I know she wants to stay here and she knows the same about me, because we have talked about just that. We could move, but that in itself is not what is important. What is important is that we know where the other stands and why!

Another example: In my first marriage, after twelve years I had decided to leave business and study for the ministry. My wife was appalled at the thought, but said little after our first discussion. I expected her to be enthusiastic about such a "noble" change. She expected me to stay in business for, as she said, "I married a businessman, not a minister." We passed in the night like two darkened ships, because early on and later, we didn't share our expectations or attempt to negotiate a compromise. Expectations need to be aired and shared and talked through. Although every marriage has two people on the bridge, the ship of marriage can only go in one direction—at one time.

There are five "expectations" that I feel need to be examined *and understood* by individuals in a marriage partnership. I'll discuss each one briefly.

EMOTIONAL EXPECTATIONS

These have a lot to do with "feelings"—about areas in your life that are difficult to articulate. You often feel silly or embarrassed to tell another person that, when you get down in the dumps, you need to be listened to and hugged; that a little praise goes a long way; that you are scared to death at times; that you are unsure about your looks or your brains; that you expect to be supported in front of your in-laws or protected in strange situations; that you want to be allowed to cry or swear; or as my cousin suggested, "When in danger or in doubt, run around and scream and shout!" Emotional expectations also go a lot deeper than these. You expect quality time with your partner. You expect to learn more about yourself and about him or her. You expect to share and be shared with. You expect an intimate relationship in which you can know that it is okay to be emotional; that it is okay to be open, okay to share your feelings as well as accept another's feelings, okay to want to deepen and broaden your marriage relationship.

Not everyone can do this, and many of you don't, and yet it is so important for the health of the marriage. Your emotional expectations are literally your "guts" and, if you don't share them, your partner is flying blind. Share them as they come to mind, without worrying about whether they make sense or not. You are not looking for agreement or even acceptance, but simply telling your partner how you feel and what you think you need emotionally.

Silence may be golden, but in this arena it can do irreparable damage. A couple I saw some years ago were in this predicament. He refused to talk or share any of his emotional expectations. She erred in the other direction by literally sharing everything, partially out of a sense of desperation. They remained separated emotionally, which may have been self-protective on his part, but it was only self-defeating in terms of their marriage. If we only weren't so afraid of what is deep inside of us!

SEXUAL EXPECTATIONS

Unless talked out, differing sexual expectations can lead to a lot of frustration and misunderstanding. What do you enjoy doing sexually? What turns you on? What turns you off? How frequently do you wish to have sex? What haven't you tried that might intrigue you? What is off limits? We are all sexual beings and we all have sexual needs! As Richard Hettinger wrote in *Living with Sex* (Seabury Press, New York, 1966), "Sex is something we are, not just something we do."

Despite all the very explicit books and films about sex, most of us are still quite naive and reticent about discussing our sexuality. Since we receive and give pleasure sexually, we need to know what pleases our partner and he or she needs to know what pleases us!

Why be afraid to admit you might like oral sex or enjoy extensive foreplay? Why be reticent to tell your partner that you are not interested in anal intercourse? Why not talk about mutual masturbation or other fondling of the genitals or breasts. *Talk about everything!* You need to be totally open about your sexual expectations. You don't have to agree one hundred percent, but if you know what the other expects *and* doesn't expect, enjoys *and* doesn't enjoy, your ability to receive and give sexual pleasure will increase a hundredfold. Whatever you both decide to do and not to do in bed is okay!

Men sometimes assume that they are expected "to perform" more than their wife either expects or desires. Unless talked out, this can lead to impotence, disinterest, or exhaustion. It is sexual quality, not quantity, that most of us want. If you can let go of your assumptions, most of which come from books, movies, and fantasies, and share your deepest yearnings and your deepest fears with the person you desire, trust, and love the most, your sexuality can become more fully and freely expressed and experienced.

SPIRITUAL EXPECTATIONS

God, in one way or another, is a factor in all our lives. You may ignore Him. You may adore Him. You may be somewhere in between. But since your spiritual or searching side is such a deep and integral part of your basic humanity, and since you do struggle with it (either as a believer, agnostic, or atheist), you need to talk to your marriage partner about what all this means or doesn't mean to you. Like sex, religion is one of the truly private realms. But also like sex, religion can cause a lot of trouble if it becomes a cause of dissent and distance, rather than an opportunity for closeness, learning, and growth.

Billy Sunday, an American evangelist (1863–1935) once said, "Going to church doesn't make you a Christian any more than going to a garage makes you an automobile." He does have a point. Don't use church or temple attendance as the be-all and end-all of "spiritual expectations." Attendance is one outward manifestation of something a lot deeper, and it is at that deeper level that you need to talk about your faith or lack of faith. I've seen individuals from different religious backgrounds and different degrees of religious enthusiasm come together, marry, and then begin a spiritual adventure together. Why? Because they respected each other enough to be open to new experiences. How? By telling each other what they did or did not believe and what they really felt about the need for some spiritual dimension to their marriage.

If you can agree with Edmund Burke, British statesman and writer (1729–1797), that, "Man is by his constitution a religious animal," you can begin to share and shape your expectations about God and you and God within your marriage partnership. You don't have to hide behind family history or personal prejudice. You shouldn't suddenly "get religion" or lose it because of what your partner's expectations seem to reflect. You should articulate what you feel and listen to what your partner feels. *God speaks through both partners!*

FAMILY EXPECTATIONS

The family is a large part of your life, and your expectations associated with it are equally huge. Outline how new family members are to be dealt with, particularly in-laws, siblings, and children in stepfamilies, and what you expect in terms of your family unit (children or no children) and the type of family existence you expect in the years ahead.

We all bring appendages with us into any marriage partnership. What are the ground rules, your own and your partner's? They don't always coincide. Who is included, and in what? And when? A couple in one of my parishes almost split up when the wife's parents came and spent a full vacation month in their little vacation house, which was paid for by the husband. In his mind it was for his immediate, not extended, family's use! In her system everyone gathered happily together. In his, vacations were distinctly separate. But they had never looked at this dilemma or their own expectations until after it had become a problem.

Couples today seem to be having smaller families and some are opting for no children at all. Whatever you and your partner decide, you must lay down some ground rules before the fact. You can always change the rules, but you cannot send the children back. Having children does not keep sick marriages together or assure you of a glowing old age. Children are not extensions of you or clones or eventual meal tickets. They are people—unique human beings—and their conception must be two things: an expression of your mutual commitment to raise them up and let them go, and a manifestation of the love you and your partner feel for each other.

My wife and I have nine wonderful children between us. When we married, we were unable for medical and age reasons to have any children together. What a blessing in disguise, for it took care of what would have been very different expectations. I probably would have wanted a baby. My wife definitely would not have. Nevertheless, we talked about it, even though it wasn't even a live possibility. The trick is "talk it out" *before* conception, when you have real choices to make, when your expectations can be translated into what is best for you *and* the children you hope to have or already have!

We all have a dream family floating around somewhere in our consciousness: two children, a country house, a dog, a flower garden, trips to the beach, Christmas with the grandparents, long evenings in front of the fire, friends, weekends. The list goes on and so do our expectations. Share these dreams, for they say a lot about what you think and long for. If your partner knows you really want to live in the suburbs and you know your partner wants to live in the city, you can face up to these different expectations before you get married. Compromises can be worked, if facts are known, but surprises can only lead to anger and recriminations. Life's expectations are very important. Talk about them, adjust them, try different modes, *and* respect each other's dreams!

FINANCIAL EXPECTATIONS

Mark Twain put it very succinctly: "The lack of money is the root of all evil!" What are your financial expectations? Is a living wage enough or are you shooting for the stars? Do you expect to become a millionaire or do you expect your spouse to become a millionaire? How important is money in terms of prestige, freedom, success, and "things"? Be honest! Be frank with each other, for out of shared financial expectations can come new balances and a new reality. He may assume she needs a big house. She might want quite the opposite. She may assume he wants to be president of General Motors. He might like to get out of a big company and start his own. He is afraid to do this or that for fear he can't meet his financial expectations, even though he has no idea what they are!

You see the dilemmas we can get into by not sharing expectations, both before the actual marriage and regularly throughout the life of the partnership?

Who is ultimately important, and what is ultimately important? These are questions to look at when you set priorities and share expectations. *The answers are within you.* God has given you the capacity to love yourself enough, to love another enough, to be open to all the promises and possibilities of life—particularly those new to your own experience!

You must set your priorities as well as take the ultimate responsibility for the quality of your life and that of your marriage partner. You are interconnected! Furthermore, you both must speak up and speak out, for it is what you both expect that moderates and measures the reality of your life together. It isn't so much agreement as comprehension. It isn't so much that your priorities and expectations match, but that you rejoice in what you agree on, accept the difference, and promise to listen and to learn from each other. Try to put each other first. Try to hear what your partner is asking of you and of the marriage. Try and change!

FEELINGS, FIGHTING, AND FORGIVING

God may forgive you, but I never can.
—QUEEN ELIZABETH I

*T*his alliteration, which sounds more like the name of a law firm than the title of a chapter, may help you remember that sharing your feelings, fighting with one another, and then forgiving one another are simply the way human animals get along! People communicate, learn, grow up, and grow closer by being human enough to experience this very natural behavior without "freaking out" or running away. Marriage partners should learn to manage these "events" with grace and with love.

FEELINGS ARE REAL

Joy, fear, wonder, anger, pain, hope, concern, caring . . . the list goes on and on. Feelings are part and parcel of what makes us human beings. Feelings may not be rational, but they are real. Feelings may be very intense and even intolerable, but they are neither right nor wrong! Feelings simply reflect what is way down deep inside of us, what moves us, motivates us, helps and impedes us. Feelings are such a vital part of us that they *must* be spoken, heard, and lived with. As Pogo, the cartoon character, said, "We have met the enemy and it is us." We must live with "US."

"I hate you" may be exactly how you feel about your spouse at 10:14 on Monday night, September the twenty-second. It is how you *feel*. It represents a lot of emotions that have bubbled to the surface, some of which have to do with him or her, some with you, some with some event that has nothing to do with either of you. You are not saying that you want a divorce or you want to kill your spouse or that you want to leave or that you want to do anything dramatically different. You just feel angry and your spouse is the focus of your anger, and he or she needs to let you share these feelings. Whether it is logical or not has nothing to do with it. It is how you feel and that is all that is important to you at this particular time. You want to be heard—to be accepted as you are and where you are. You are hurting and that pain and anger needs to get out, if healing is to follow. "If you can't yell, you'll feel like Hell!"

I ran across this quote from an "unknown author" in a paper put out by the Benedict Labre House in Montreal. In it he writes, "Please listen carefully and try to hear what I am not saying, what I'd like to be able to say, what for survival I need to say, but what I can't say. . . . You've got to help me. You've got to hold out your hand."

In other words, please FEEL along with me, know at least

that I'm feeling up or down or whatever. We are so literal when someone else speaks out and so unaware when we are the ones doing the talking. Why?

Individuals do have a right to their feelings, an obligation to let them out, *and* the responsibility to work them through. Otherwise we get depressed. Timing and caution are important but, like an upset stomach, feelings need to be "thrown up." When that can happen we fell better, act better, and are better able to deal with the root cause of our malaise. You don't really "hate" your spouse but you needed to say that in order to open your windows and let the real reasons for your discomfort emerge. Your partner may have had very little to do with it!

LEARN TO DEAL WITH FEELINGS

There is nothing more difficult than learning to deal with feelings. Since it is such a touchy area, you need to develop some ground rules that will allow and encourage the sharing of feelings, so that your marriage partnership can be strengthened—not damaged. Remember that what comes out can be dealt with. What stays buried festers like a boil. Take a look at and practice these four guidelines.

1. Don't take everything your partner says *personally*. You are not—repeat not—at the center of his or her thoughts twenty-four hours a day. If he doesn't like where you had dinner, it most likely has to do with the quality of the food, not your choice of the restaurant. If you say you don't like her relatives, that has more to do with them than it does with you.

2. Do take everything your partner says *seriously*. That is how he or she feels, whether it pleases or interests you or not. His saying "You don't care" means he *feels* you don't care, even though you may think you've been kind or considerate beyond measure. It has little to do with you, but we all tend to be so narcissistic, we can hardly bear to admit this. It is this self-absolution that impedes your looking beyond his words and into his heart.

3. Don't take everything your partner says *literally*. Words mean different things to different people at different times. "If you love me, you would do this or that." "I can't stand your children." "I don't like you." "You don't know what you are talking about." "I feel you don't care whether I live or die." "If you loved me, you would never do that or say that again." Examine these and similar expressions of feelings both as the speaker and the hearer. We don't literally mean everything we say, so why should you only hear what he or she says as a literal statement of fact?

4. Before you say anything, think it through—bite your tongue—count to ten. You want to be heard by your partner. Therefore, present your views calmly and carefully. A few seconds of caution can save hours of pain.

The main thing about feelings is that they should be heard, aired, shared, respected, talked about, and worked through. Real intimacy, which I think is the bedrock of any successful marriage partnership, is largely due to two people loving each other enough and trusting each other enough to feel safe enough to share deep, deep feelings without fear of criticism, rejections, *or* loss of love.

WHAT KIND OF FIGHTER ARE YOU?

Dr. Eric Berne wrote a book entitled *Games People Play* (Grove Press, New York, 1964). In it he had a chapter entitled "Now I've Got You, You Son of a Bitch."

Believe it or not, this is a favorite couple's game! Why? Well I guess our instinctive response is so often visceral. When we feel threatened from the slightest sniff of attack, we often strike out or slap back. And to make sure "our rights" are protected, we try "to get" whoever has had the temerity to affront us! This sounds ridiculous and it really is, but there is "fight" in each of us and it needs to be managed.

Couples who do fight fairly and carefully are healthier than couples who bury their hostility because someone once told them that "married people shouldn't fight." That is bad advice. A couple I know, who are splitting up after many years together, couldn't or wouldn't fight because of an old wives' tale like that. What happened? Their anger got pushed back inside and then, since it had to come out in one way or another, it seeped out in devious, harmful, hurtful, and inappropriate ways. She had affairs with men; he had an affair with his job. They put each other down in public and in ways that made you not want to be with them.

Fighting can be cathartic! Fighting is also an art. Fighting should neither be encouraged nor discouraged, for each individual and couple must develop their own means of resolving conflict. Nevertheless, you need to know with whom you are dealing when you get into a feud for there are different kinds of fighters. There are aggressive fighters, passive fighters, dirty fighters, sex and money fighters, dangerous fighters, and what I would categorize as healthy fighters.

1. An *aggressive* fighter tends to look for trouble and picks fights. Feisty is one description; pugnacious is another! An aggressive fighter escalates and attacks and seems to want to win an immediate victory or at the very least an admission of wrong doing by the partner.
2. A *passive* fighter fights back by doing and saying very little. His or her silence is their greatest weapon and it can be enormously effective. Haven't we all been driven up the wall by someone who just sits there and looks and doesn't say or do a thing?
3. A *dirty* fighter dredges up the past, whether or not it has anything to do with the disagreement at hand. A dirty fighter attacks our ego, our sense of integrity, our dignity by using words and tactics that tear us down and lay us low. A dirty fighter threatens to leave. A dirty fighter goes for the jugular.
4. A *sex and money* fighter uses these extraordinarily powerful weapons to win, but in the final analysis, usually loses. Withholding sex or money is like a terrorist attack. We don't know how to respond, so we often lose our cool and lash out in blind response. The initiator is distanced and so are we, the net effect being a broken relationship that takes a lot of "eating crow" and time and regrets and maybe even more reprisals before it can be reestablished. We

should not use our sexuality or our net worth as a means to win a battle. We might very easily lose the war!

5. A *dangerous* fighter is violent, emotionally as well as physically. His rage is uncontrollable and he lashes out in ways that can do permanent harm to his victims and to himself! *People who are physically abused must call the police! There is absolutely no excuse for spouse abuse at any time.*

6. A *healthy* fighter accepts conflict as a normal event in any intimate human relationship, but doesn't seek it out. If a fight ensues, the healthy fighter tries to "keep it in the yard" and bring it to a conclusion as soon as both partners have had their say. The temptation to have the last word or to win can be overwhelming, which means you must keep your cool, your balance, and your love for your "opposing partner."

BE DIRECT WITH EACH OTHER

If your spouse is mad about the fact that Joe Jones seemed over-attentive to you at the Smiths' party, he needs to say *that* and not talk about the lousy food or that you shouldn't go out on weeknights. If you are troubled by his drinking and the change it makes in his personality, say *that*, and not that he's gaining weight and that one way to lose it is to drink less or switch to wine. No one likes direct confrontation, but believe me, it is far better for the tomorrows.

Sharing feelings can lead to fights, but that is better than no sharing at all. Fighting also can lead to forgiveness, which can make a marriage well again.

THE ART OF FORGIVING

In the sixteenth century Queen Elizabeth I was reported to have said, "God may forgive you but I never can." Most of us have a terrible time swallowing our pride, overlooking slights, and forgiving other human beings for being human beings! George Herbert, Anglican priest and poet of the seventeenth century, gently leads us toward reality when he says: "He that cannot forgive others breaks the bridge over which he himself must pass if he would ever reach heaven; for everyone has a need to be forgiven."

Little slights can turn into enormous mountains of resentment and any thought of forgiveness is driven from our minds. I knew a husband who fell into this trap by being insensitive to his wife's pleas to be noticed, to be taken seriously, to be appreciated as an attractive woman. She even told him about other men who had said how attractive she was—partially to make him jealous but more to make him notice her. She became obsessed with this and so angry that anything he did was open territory for criticism. He finally said something that made her realize that he did care and care a lot but by that time she had closed down. It took a lot of time and stroking on his part to get her to accept his limitations and to begin to forgive him. She told me it was the most difficult emotional experience she had been through—to hate and love the same man at the same time—and then to begin to accept his limitations and forgive his shortcomings.

Human beings make mistakes—lots of them, in fact. People who love each other do stupid and insensitive things. Look in your own mirror! If you can overlook your own bunglings, can you not also forgive the bunglings of another—especially the one you profess to love so much? Can you be mature enough to remember that his or her particular action has to do with his or her situation, need at the moment, crisis, or whatever, and nothing to do with you? Somehow we tend to not be able to let go of the notion that we have been personally attacked!

Okay. Forgive, but don't forget! That may help, for it is very difficult to completely forget a personal slight or injury. The scars sometimes last for a lifetime. If you have to hang on to the fact that something has happened, *but* forgive the someone who made it happen, the pressure is eased and the pain may eventually recede. I knew a woman who was unable to forgive her husband for having an office affair—an affair which in fact was never consummated sexually. He simply had found someone at the office whom he could "talk to" and he told his wife exactly that. She focused on the so-called infidelity, instead of trying to forgive him, appreciating his honesty with her, taking a look at herself and what made him seek an outside ear in the first place. Their marriage came within inches of breaking apart. What saved it was their willingness to talk it out with a third party who put both sides, both errors in judgment, into a different perspective. They both finally conceded they were both wrong, which allowed them to resume a dialogue not laced with recriminations and to begin to regroup and recommit to their marriage.

To forgive your partner in marriage can sometimes be extraordinarily difficult. But it is not impossible, and it is crucial to your relationship. The exercise that follows might help you to sort out what stands in your way.

EXERCISE 5

1. Ask yourself what happened to make you so angry? Did you have any part in it?
2. Was "it" directed at you personally?
3. Is "it" a vital issue, an oversight, or just an annoyance?
4. Are "they" sorry—in deed as well as word?
5. Have you been frank about how you feel?
6. Have they explained why they did this?
7. Do you want to forgive them?
8. Will you forgive them? (For our sake, the answer here should be yes!)

A friend of mine once said that the best way to win a tug-of-war is to "let go of the rope." I feel the best way to win almost anything and insure happiness and strengthen your marriage partnership is to let go of your hurt and forgive. Try it! You won't like it at first, but in turn, you'll reap its rewards. Your forgiveness of another allows them in turn and in time to forgive you. As the African proverb says, "He who forgives ends the quarrel."

CARE, TRUST, AND RESPECT

Teach us to care and not to care.
—T. S. ELIOT
Ash-Wednesday

T.S. Eliot's admonition is a good thought to hang on to as you plunge into the more complicated waters of how to care for, trust in, and respect your partner for life. Times change more than people, which means you need to develop, early on, the kind of behavior that can withstand the temptations and turmoil of the passing years. *Care* is a word like love. It can be used for selfish, as well as unselfish, ends. *Trust* is a concept that is so central to any relationship that, once broken, it takes years to repair. *Respect* is something we all desire, yet you must give it as well! The three are very much interrelated.

CARE FOR YOURSELF

To care for your spouse you must first care for yourself! That may sound selfish, but it isn't. Look at it another way. How can you give to your partner what you don't possess yourself? If you don't care for yourself, how can you possibly care for your partner? So often many of us, especially in the helping professions, are so busy "helping" or "caring" for others that we don't properly care for ourselves *or* our families! This gets back to priorities. This gets back to who is important and why. "Caring" for my parishioners by working fourteen hours a day may make me feel good, my family feel bad, and those I'm caring for confused. Unless my house is in order, it is obvious to everyone else that something is amiss— and it is me! To go even further with this, if I become worried about you, because you are tired and working far too hard, your "caring" for me becomes a burden on me rather than a help—another worry on top of everything else! Can you see the vicious cycle?

There was a story about a woman who was always caring for and helping everyone else, even when they didn't want such attention! They say the way you could tell who she was currently caring for and helping was by their hunted look!

You must care for yourself first. I don't mean wanton self-indulgence, but a sensible caring for your body and your mind and your soul. A therapist I worked with helped me develop this list:

1. Relax.
2. Enjoy.
3. Be creative.

4. Be useful.
5. Be thoughtful.
6. Be thankful.

Notice where "be thoughtful" or caring for others is and where "relax and enjoy" or caring for yourself is? This list of priorities works, at least for me. Those I live with have commented how much nicer I have become, how much more caring, in the best sense of that word, since I am more available, less obsessive, and more in tune with the world and the people with whom I interact every day.

As children, we were taught to use our hand as a guide to prayer, starting with our thumb and working around to the little finger. The thumb was for Praise, then came Thanksgiving, then Penitence, then Intercession, and last *and* least, our little finger, which stood for Petition or prayer for ourself. No wonder we have it all backwards. As I have grown in years and understanding and faith, I've come to realize that, if I cannot be open with God about myself and my problems, how can I possibly pray for others and their problems? I must clear my own decks before I try to help you with yours. Caring begins at home—in our hearts and in our minds. "Love your neighbor as yourself" says the writer of Leviticus in the Old Testament, and Jesus echoes it and reinterprets it in the New. Know ourselves. Love ourselves. Care for ourselves. Then and only then can we take on the world.

BE NO ONE'S SAVIOR

"Caring" and "saving" are very different words and concepts. It is fine to care for someone you love, *but* you must not try to be their "Savior," and here are five reasons why you shouldn't:

1. They already have one.
2. You cannot save them.
3. You have no right to try to lead their lives for them.
4. You are not them nor can you possibly know all the dynamics of their situation.
5. They—not you—must make the first move.

Worrying openly and excessively about someone else means, in essence, that they don't have to worry as much *and* shows that you don't really care about them getting better. If you did, you'd leave them alone. You try to take the problem out of the only hands that can fix it—theirs! That old German proverb, "Charity sees the need, not the cause" is so applicable here. Help others help themselves. Don't try to second guess them. Focus on the need you have been asked to help with, not the individual you have *not* been asked to save!

PUT YOUR PARTNER FIRST

You should care for your partner more than you care for your guests! It is amazing and appalling, but we often give those we love the most a lot less attention than those we care about least. Watch your behavior before, during, and after a party.

Who do you preen for? Who are you nice to? Who do you forgive first for lateness or rudeness or for drinking too much? Caring for others is a good thing and it can enrich and deepen your caring at home, but be sensitive to how critical you can be of those nearest and dearest to you. Working out your own frustrations and feelings of inadequacy with your marriage partner may be appropriate under certain circumstances, but do not call it "caring."

CARE FOR PEOPLE AS THEY ARE

This may be the hardest part of all, to care for people as they are and where they are. In the Biblical story of Zacchaeus, Jesus cared. Jesus accepted Zacchaeus. Jesus chose to have dinner with the least likely candidate in Jericho! But that's the point. Behind every facade, every put-off, every outward barrier, there lurks a child of God—a human creature who has the same basic needs that we do—to be accepted, cared for, liked, loved, held, and respected.

Sometimes, if you can break through the coverings and "see" and "hear" how they feel and why, a whole new dimension will unfold.

Caring is so important. How you care or are cared for tells volumes about who you love and how you love. Caring is literally love in action.

TRUST: THE CORE INGREDIENT

An antonym for trust is doubt, and that is exactly what creeps into a marriage relationship that lacks this core ingredient, this measure of integrity, this protection from the winds of change and challenge. To put it bluntly, a marriage partnership cannot continue if the ingredient called "trust" is no longer there.

Trust takes a long time to set firmly in its foundations. Trusting others easily or with difficulty has a lot to do with your past experience and upbringing. If those you have trusted from the past have kept their contracts, it takes less time for you to make new contracts. If you have been betrayed, it is a long, long road back. I once gave a fellow clergyman some confidential, pastoral insights about a parishioner. He took that information and took advantage of that individual. On every other level I liked him, but I'll not forget this incident, nor shall I ever trust him again. That is sad, but true. Trust cannot be abused without grave consequences.

In one of *Aesop's Fables* the moral is, "Never trust a friend who deserts you in a pinch." When you feel deserted or betrayed by another, particularly one near and dear to you, the damage done to your ego, your sense of fairness, your integrity, your personhood, your love is enormous. One partner having an "affair" is the best marital example I know. One partner stealing from the other is the best business example I know. Trust is broken no matter what explanation is offered. An empty, helpless, alone feeling replaces the almost indescribable unity true partners should enjoy. Once lust or opportunism, or whatever causes one to want to break this basic rule, raises its ugly head, watch out. Slow down, take a cold shower, stay away from the office, do anything and everything to avoid duplicity. It is not only unfair to your partner, it is very unhealthy for you.

WHAT TRUSTING MEANS

Most of what I have said thus far about trust has been negative, but that is to underline how serious any disruption of the trust relationship between two people can be. In these days of conflicting stories, public lying, and sleazy behavior, trust becomes even more vital. Just to be able to trust someone enough to be able to believe them unequivocably is a wonderful thing. When a person's deeds equal what they say, it proves the old adage, "Our word *is* our honor." Honor and trust are synonymous!

Here is what I mean when I say "I trust you" to my wife and with some variation to my family and my friends. It is almost a creed for marriage—for it is that important!

- I trust you means I believe what you say. I believe you believe it also.
- I trust you means I believe what you say is what you will do, unless you tell me otherwise.
- I trust you means I know you'll make mistakes, but that they will be honest ones.
- I trust you means I can tell you anything and know you'll keep and guard that information with your life.

- I trust you means I can count on you being there when I need you.
- I trust you means I know you are faithful to me, mentally and physically.
- I trust you means I know you truly love me.

RESPECT BETWEEN PARTNERS

Respecting another when their views on a particular subject are far apart from yours is not that easy, but it does show a caring, an openness, and a maturity that is a wonderful and winsome example of what I would call "shared humanity." My wife and I are well read, opinionated, vocal people, but we have learned (with battle scars and gray hairs to prove it) to respect where the other is coming from and what they are trying to get across. Respect is being able to listen to and accept another person's opinions on any subject at any time without "losing it" or losing them. We don't have to agree. We don't even have to listen for very long. But we do have to respect that person and their right to their opinion. Such "respect" is important for our marriage partnership for it allows us not only to be ourselves but allows others the same privilege!

Respect has other dimensions as well. Respect your partner as a unique individual—one of a kind—who cannot be packaged or put on a shelf. Respect his or her rights as a human being and respect that he or she is not an extension of you or a clone of anyone else. Respect his or her integrity. Respect his or her privacy and the need to be alone and do things without you. Respect "the hard to believe fact" that he or she is different from you—that you talk differently, think differently, act differently. One of the healthy dynamics of a healthy marriage partnership is how such differences are managed.

CONSIDER THE ALTERNATIVES

Another way to look at this is to consider the alternatives. Someone you don't respect is usually someone who has no openness, no opinions to measure, no individuality to react with—no personality to challenge us. Imagine being married to a blob. In another scenario, someone you can't respect is someone who is amoral or immoral or who plays by a totally different set of rules. Imagine being married to a sleaze.

Respect between partners in marriage and business is earned and maintained by "the record." Like trust, it is easier to lose than to gain, and like trust, respect grows with experience. Unlike trust, which is more like a beam holding up a house, respect grows and changes as events unfold. The child who earns an athletic letter or the spouse who goes back to school or the parent who changes careers earns new respect. My wife is a psychotherapist and I have enormous respect for her professional competence. It is not based just on blind love, but on "the results" of her practice. She also respects me!

Respect is not flattery, but fact, as seen by the observer. Respect is taking your partner seriously!

To care, to trust, to respect—three signs along the marriage road. Three short words and three simple concepts, but not that easy to practice in real life. "Care for me and I'll care for you" is not enough. "Trust me" is not enough. It is our actions that help the truster and the trustee turn these words into the reality both seek. "Respect me" is the cry in all of our hearts, for we so desperately want to be thought well of. But we must first learn to respect ourselves. It is out of your own confidence that you can have confidence in another person *and* in the differences between you.

HARD WORK, FAITH, AND FUN

God gives every bird its food, but he does not throw it into the nest.

—JOSIAH GILBERT HOLLAND

*I*pair these first two words, *work* and *faith*, because when I was growing up they seemed to be the poles of existence and the fundamental movements of life. If you worked hard at your job and had faith in yourself, in God, and in others, you would succeed! I know now that life isn't that simple or compartmentalized. Yet there is something to be said for such a dual focus—a focus on what can be accomplished within us and through the movement of God's people and of God himself. The third word, *fun*, is one of the rewards that hard work and faith spawn. Obviously, marriages are not all "fun and games," but if they aren't "fun" in large measure, something is dreadfully amiss.

NOT A MAGICAL MYSTERY TOUR

Any partnership—business, legal, or marital—requires an enormous amount of work, if it is to be successful. Look at the hours that people put in to balance their books or take inventory or complete a brief or whatever needs to be done to keep the enterprise going. It is hard and constant work; some of it drudgery, some fun, some stimulating, some extremely tiring. No one assumes a business can succeed without WORK; working in it, working at it, working with it. Why, then, do we expect a marriage to be any different? Is it simple? No. Is it easy? No. Does it automatically succeed? No. *Then is there a difference?* Yes. The difference is in the way we regard marriage. We treat marriage as a magical mystery tour. It is supposed to work somehow on its own—without work. We must know somewhere way down deep that that is ridiculous!

If you only could see the parallels, rather than the differences, between marriage and other endeavors. If you only could see how similar successful partnerships are, whether they be business, legal, *or* marital. The common ingredient of hard work is vital to the growth, maintenance, and success of them all.

SEARCH FOR EXCELLENCE

In their book *Search for Excellence* (Thomas J. Peters and Robert H. Waterman Jr., Harper and Row, 1982), Peters and

Waterman tell us that excellent companies seem to have several things in common:

- They are brilliant on the basics.
- Within them intellect does not overpower wisdom.
- They work hard to keep things simple in a complex world.
- They persist.
- They insist on top quality.
- They fawn on their customers.
- They treat employees like adults.

Translate these business observations into marriage terms and they make perfect sense. Working their list backward:

- You need to act like adults.
- You should fawn over your spouses, as if they were customers.
- You should aim high and expect the best in your marriage relationship.
- You should hang in there through all the inevitable ups and downs.
- You should keep the marriage simple yet deep.
- You should be wise rather than fast with the tongue.
- You should focus on what is important and basic to the partnership itself.

It's easy to say, you might be thinking, but *how* should I go about it? I hope these five guidelines are of help:

1. Heed Peter Drucker's advice and "think smarter not faster." Use your brain, not your mouth *or* feet!

2. Spend the time necessary and appropriate to building and maintaining a deep relationship (and I would wager that this is more time than you are spending now!). Just as I cannot be on top of things at the store when I am somewhere else, I cannot know the needs and aspirations of my spouse, if I'm always at the office or glued to the TV when I am at home.

3. Take your partner as seriously as you take yourself *and* as seriously as you would like him or her to take you.

4. Enjoy the ups, learn from the downs, and do not let them go to your head or get you down. A healthy partnership has its ripples and misunderstandings. It is how they are put into perspective and lived through and worked out that tells the real story.

5. Use the support systems available to you to broaden and deepen your partnership as if your "economic future" depended on the outcome. This puts it on a par with your pocketbook—the great motivator! You may need to talk to your clergyman or to go for individual therapy or get family counseling or seek financial/career advice *or* whatever will help! When you have a toothache, you rush to the dentist; when you have a chest pain, to an internist. What is the difference when you have marriage pains? *You must get the help you need!*

This can be very difficult, for it doesn't come easily or naturally. As Josiah Gilbert Holland wrote, "God gives every bird its food, but he does not throw it into the nest." You must work hard for what is valuable and necessary for your well-being. You must work hard to improve your communications, whether they be emotional or practical or sexual. You must work hard to keep yourself and your partnership tough and tender, balanced yet free, informed, healthy, deep, and fun!

FAITH: THE FORCE OF LIFE

Faith is central and crucial to an idea, an enterprise, a marriage, and, obviously, God. Faith requires a choice, and that is not easy to make *or* to maintain. Leo Tolstoy said, "Faith is the force of life," and he was right. Faith involves tremendous energy. Faith undergirds whatever significant commitment we have made, and because of that requires a lot of hard work. It may well be "the ear of the soul," to borrow from that second-century theologian Clement of Alexandria, but it also bridges the gap between reality and hope, the present and the future, what is in place and what we want to accomplish.

Faith is seeing the opportunities *before* getting caught up in the inevitable problems. Faith—whether it be in a business or marriage or in God—requires "a leap," a commitment, a willingness to buy in and stick with it, at least for a period of time long enough to make a careful and reasoned determination. Someone said to the Rev. John Wesley, founder of the Methodist Movement, "Live by faith until you have faith." In other words, be open to the possibilities and the promises of faith. Give faith time to root and to grow and to blossom. In the following paragraphs I will talk about our inherent spirituality. But here let me focus on faith in "business" and "marriage," for, if you accept the fact that there are similarities in these partnerships, you can see how "faith" is an important ingredient in both arenas.

Business	*Marriage*
I must have faith in the product I make and sell.	I must have faith in the institution of marriage I have bought into.
I must have faith in my fellow workers.	I must have faith in my marriage partner.
I must have faith that we can make and sell the best product anywhere.	I must have faith that our marriage will flower and flourish in its own unique way.
I must have faith that disappointments and setbacks can be dealt with and will be overcome.	I must have faith that we will survive the inevitable ups and downs inherent in any marriage relationship.
I must have faith that I am with people who want to and will work with me.	I must have faith that my partner is as committed to our marriage as I am.

See how they correspond and how interchangeable "faith" is whether you are dealing with how you make your living or the quality of your personal life.

FAITH IS BELIEVING

Some anonymous wag wrote, "Faith is believing what you know ain't so." That's funny and somewhat true, because faith in what is ahead of you does test your credibility at times! It is easier to deal with faith in the more mundane terms, as we did when we compared business to marriage. But faith in a personal God, a God who is at the center of your being, as well as your entire existence, takes a very different kind of plunge. You still have to jump, but it is often a lot further. You might be able to control how you jump, but not how you land. This is where we all have difficulty, because we have lost control in a sense. But we also gain something far greater—a confidence that whatever else happens along the way, we are not alone or forgotten. In the midst of all his incredible troubles, Job said, "I know that my Redeemer lives." The writer of the Letter to the Hebrews reminds us that "Faith is the substance of things hoped for, the evidence of things not seen."

I cannot know what the consumer market will do tomorrow, but I can have faith enough to believe my product is basically sound and that it will continue to sell. I cannot possibly know what might affect my life next week, but I can have faith enough in my marriage, regardless of what might bruise it—a misunderstanding or a mishap or even a serious mistake—to know that it will survive and be the better for it. I cannot know exactly or definitely what will happen to me or my body or my soul after I close my eyes in death, but my faith tells me that "All will be well" and that I will be in God's loving hands.

There is a story of a young German sailor who was lost at sea during World War I. His last letter to his mother ended with these words: "If you hear that my ship has been torpedoed, do not fear, for the seas into which my body sinks are in the hands of my Savior, from which nothing can separate me." *That is faith!*

FUN IS LIKE TONIC

Fun is an elusive concept, for it means different things to different people. Fun for me may be drudgery for you. What I think is a funny story may be unfunny to you. Humor has many facets, too. But what I am talking about here is the fun two married individuals have because of their special and unique relationship.

If marriage is a grind, something is very wrong. You should enjoy being together and have fun in your marriage. Having fun together can take multiple forms. Just because she has fun working in the yard doesn't automatically mean he will like it too. Just because he has fun watching sports on TV doesn't mean she will too. These are two very real examples of where assumptions can drain the fun right out of an otherwise good relationship.

It is a right and good thing for individuals in a marriage partnership to have individual fun, as well as "corporate" fun, but the two need to be kept clearly defined and separate. Togetherness is great, but not all the time. In fact, too much togetherness can drive the fun right out of a marriage. Healthy partners may have fun doing some things alone, some things with their friends, and other things with their partner. All are okay. All are necessary. All can nurture a good marriage. It is a sign of real maturity and a deep love to accept and know these differences.

My wife and I have a lot of fun dancing, but for everyday exercise, she prefers to walk and I prefer to jog. She has great fun "visiting" with friends and family. I have more fun doing things with them. I enjoy shopping, she doesn't. We both enjoy reading. We have fun working together in the garden;

she plants and waters; I mow and dig. We have fun working on our house and entertaining our friends. We do not have fun counseling together, even though we are both in the "helping professions." We have a lot of fun just being together! The list goes back and forth and on and on. The reason for this personal litany is to show that having fun can and should have multiple expressions. We've worked it out through trial and error. An easier way might have been to sit down and talk about our preferences and differences and likenesses. Here is an exercise that should help.

EXERCISE 6
To Each His Fun

Think of as many answers as you can to the following questions:

1. What is fun for me?
2. What is fun for my partner?
3. What is fun for us?
4. What might be fun for us in the future?

A list such as this can help to remind you of necessary balances and the complicated experiences of being full partners in a marriage. Fun is like tonic. It enhances the gin, but doesn't dilute it!

Fun can sometimes not be funny, can even be dangerous, hence these warnings!

1. When your partner does something that he or she thinks is fun or funny, but that you find offensive (such as a sick

joke), you need to tell them. Don't hesitate. Don't wait. If you do, they are none the wiser and you become a lot angrier.

2. "Fun" at someone else's expense, particularly your partner's, is a "no-no," as well as a dangerous and unfair game.

3. Fun that excludes another, such as a weekend where four people go off and play tennis, leaving the fifth out, is neither fun nor funny.

4. Fun cannot be forced. It needs to flow from an attitude that is relaxed and one that encourages enjoyment.

Fun can enrich a marriage a hundredfold! Fun can be the tonic that allows each of you to shed the pressures of everyday living. Fun can be the latch that opens windows into a world where work does not come first, but marriage partners do! Have fun, have faith, and work hard—these three admonitions are passed on because they are vital to a good and productive marriage. I know, for they are central to my own!

CHANGE AND EVOLUTION

The ever-whirling wheel of change; the
which all mortal things doth sway

—EDMUND SPENSER
(The Faerie Queene)

*B*elieve it or not we do change! We change for the better and we change for the worse. I have found in my own case that I am far more aware of and interested in what other people think than I was twenty years ago. Conversely, I am more intolerant of the intolerant, which is a besetting sin in itself! Change is an up and down, in and out process, and it is what evolves in our attitudes and behavior that is the real measure of our maturity. My wife tells me that I am easier to live with than I was five years ago but that I tend to overact to new situations as I get older. Our evolution into more sensitive and realistic human beings has a direct bearing on the health of our marriage partnerships.

Partners can help each other change—not only bad habits or unhelpful attitudes—but in evolving into better people.

CHANGE TO HEALTHY

People change. Love changes. Circumstances change. Inside feelings and outside happenings change us for better *and* worse. It is how you recognize, manage, and accept change that keeps you sane and involved in partnership. Change is threatening, but it is healthy. Look at how you "loved" your partner when you first were swept off your feet or how he or she loved you. Would you really care to have remained in that state, just as it was then, when you are where you are now? Definitely not, at least I wouldn't. If you really think about it and are honest with yourself, you are glad you have changed, particularly when that change has broadened and deepened your life, your love, and your partnership.

You can change in negative ways too. But these are harder to recognize. You can get fat. You can drink too much. You can become workaholics or sportaholics. You can become paranoid or depressed or jealous or just plain angry. These changes are not healthy, but you need the wisdom and the will to do something about them when you or those you love the most are "swimming away from the dock."

Change can be made in two directions, into and out of gear. The willingness to change for the better and the ability to spot change for the worse are measures of your maturity, your love for yourself and your partner, and your commitment to the marriage. Age, moods, attraction, health, and job changes beset and bewilder all of us. The first moves at its own speed, the others have much to do with our individual circumstances. But in each case change is inevitable. Here are some major life changes we all face.

AGE CHANGE

We all get older, and with age comes changes in appearance, energy level, agility, patience, and outlook in general. You can fight them and lose them or accept them and learn to live within their confines gracefully and gratefully. Seeking eternal youth is not only foolish, it robs you of the particular enjoyments different ages bring. You should stay in shape, but not in constant competition with the neighbors or your children. You should enjoy sex, but not try to act half your age in bed. You should work hard, but a little less each year, rather than a little more in the false hope that it will make you more indispensable. You should relax and enjoy and embrace each phase of life—from no children to children to the empty nest and on to grandchildren. The maturation process, when viewed from age fifty, makes more sense than when viewed from twenty. All I can promise you is that life and love does improve with age, *if* you are willing to be yourself, not someone younger or more beautiful or smarter or whatever, *and* if you accept your partner's aging as a plus and not a minus. Believe me, it is a lot more fun to share the problems and the possibilities of age with someone you love so much you barely notice their wrinkles.

MOOD CHANGE

There is a T-shirt in a local store that has emblazoned across its front, "I'm entitled to be grumpy." I may buy it for I find that I am less tolerant and more grumpy as I get older! Our moods do change for a lot of reasons: aging, health, pressures, circumstances, job, kids, family life, spouse relationships, to name a few. The crucial thing is to be open and ready and willing to learn from these normative stages of our development.

1. Learn to recognize when your mood does change.
2. Figure out why.
3. Deal with it yourself and, if that does not work, get some professional help.
4. Do not dump it on your marriage partner or whoever else happens to be in range.

We all get down in the mouth or grumpy or out of sorts. It is our system's way of dealing with what we wish we didn't have to deal with: criticism, rejection real or imagined, etc. These are usually temporary dips. However, if you remain in an angry and depressed state you should seek outside help to help put your mood in perspective. Continual turbulence is damaging to you, to your partner, and to all who cross your path.

Moods reflect feelings and, if feelings are allowed to come out and are taken seriously, then the mood itself often improves! Look at moods as storm warnings. You can't necessarily prevent the storm from passing through, but you can prepare for it and be prepared as well for the sunlight that invariably will follow.

ATTRACTION CHANGE

When you are courting, even when you are getting "long in the tooth," sexual attraction is very powerful indeed. When you are married it moderates a bit, for cohabitation is naturally less stimulating than "stay-overs" or vacations. You don't necessarily lose your basic attraction to your partner or your attractiveness to him or her. It is just that you are more relaxed and realistic. You may be intrigued by your partner's mind, but take his acumen and intelligence more for granted, as you are exposed to it day by day. Isn't this natural and healthy? What if you were operating at a fever pitch all the time? You do lose the idealized attraction, but in its place is something far deeper.

As you grow up and old with another human being to whom you are deeply attracted, you should see him or her more as a wonderfully complete person whose body and beauty, wit and wisdom are infinitely more fascinating as time marches on. I've seen couples in their eighties who couldn't keep their eyes off each other; others whose passage through life together is like watching a marvelous play with scene after scene showing the changing, moving dynamics of two people who are attracted to each other in ever-changing ways.

Attraction can also wane. Your idealized attraction may have to give place to a diminished attraction that is different but that can, if understood, provide a continuing connection with the one whom you still care about a great deal. You may want to be alone more or your interest in sex may diminish, but that does not mean your partnership can't be retuned to adapt to these quite natural changes.

HEALTH CHANGES

Health changes are unavoidable and sometimes inexplicable. What you bargained for when you get married may not be quite what you end up with, for as we get older, our bodies get out of sync and out of tune. Sometimes even in our youth when we least expect it, we or our partner may get sick in a variety of ways. That's the real world. You can take good care of yourself and give up bad habits, but we all stand a chance of being affected and afflicted healthwise in ways that test our mettle and our marriage.

The most I can say in a few words, just touching on this extraordinarily important factor in partnerships, has to do with attitude. Your attitude toward yourself when you become ill and your partner when he or she becomes ill is a definite factor "in getting better" in the broadest sense of that word. Becoming ill begets fear and fear begets defensiveness and defensiveness begets a degree of irrational thinking and acting. *But* in the final analysis you are the one "in control." A friend of mine recently developed colon cancer, and it threw him for a loop because it was inoperable. But his words to me were "Damn it. I've got this lousy disease and I don't know what it will do to me and when, BUT I am going to be in charge—not of how long I have to live but as to the quality of the life that I am now engaged in." He took control of what he could control and it has changed his outlook and helped him cope with the disease.

It is amazing to me to observe how people often accept huge changes in their partners' mental outlooks and then literally freak out when they witness a bodily change. We do wear down and we do wear out! We have heart attacks and we do get cancer. It may not be fair, but it is fact, and the fact that a change has overcome someone you love should draw you closer, rather than drive you away. One way to put it in perspective is to consider how "I" would like to be treated as "I" grow old, weaker, and sicker. Your partner deserves no less!

JOB CHANGE

Job changes, whether they be career moves, children leaving the nest, a vocational switch, or retirement, can be very unsettling and upsetting. Our identities are so wrapped up in "what we do" that we need to monitor job change and be tolerant as adjustments are made.

The man who talks about not being able to wait for his sixty-fifth birthday may actually be scared to death of what will happen when it arrives. The woman who says she can't wait for the last child to leave home may be looking at desperate loneliness and loss of purpose. A promotion at work may also bring an unwelcome location change; a lateral move may trigger a real adjustment in how you match up realities with dreams. Partners who are sensitive to each other's ambitions and who dare to be the voice of reason, partners who can transmit their love and acceptance, particularly when the other partner is dealing with a vocational change, partners who can just "be there" as lover, friend, listener, adviser, reminder, motivator, and calmer-downer—partners like these can guide the partnership through these conflicting and confusing times.

Another way to cope with all this is to realize that the partnership itself is a job, a task in which two committed, caring people are involved, and within which significant changes take place every day. How you deal with internal partnership problems says a lot about how you deal with outside changes and pressures. *Start within and work out*—not the other way around!

THE EVOLUTIONARY STAGES OF LIFE

Darwin's theory of evolution, the survival of the fittest, may have marriage partnership ramifications! The fittest in this context seem to be those who understand the evolution of human beings from newborn babies to very old persons. Some lives are short-circuited, but most of us live a span of time and, within each section of that span, certain characteristics are exhibited that must be understood and dealt with.

Partners of the same vintage have an easier time, I think, because similar things happen to them at similar times. If you're slim and trim while he or she is beginning to sag, that can be tough to take, but if you are both exhausted after the grandchildren have visited for a week, then your "evolving" is more easily accepted.

Look at these evolutionary stages of life. From your own experience and from what you've learned from others, note some of the characteristics of these "periods."

Young adult (20–30 years old): Ambitious, romantic, selfish, idealistic, inquisitive, driven . . .

Maturing adult (30–45 years old): Job centered, success oriented, child rearer, experimenter . . .

Middle-aged adult (45–60 years old): Behavior adjustments, plateauing, looking at life and work in different ways, attitude changes, family involvement, thoughtful, more careful . . .

Older adult (60–70 years old): Retirement adjustments, starting over without protection of a job, different life and place of living, desire to explore, apathy, energy and health changes . . .

Aging adult (70–85 years old): Health and money concerns, enjoyment of senior status, more self-centered, extended family involvement, loss of confidence, grumpy at times . . .

Old adult (85–100 years old): Tired, reflective, alert, forgetful, "getting ready" . . .

You can expand or change and adjust this list. You can

expand, change, and adjust yourself because you *can* evolve in new and innovative and productive ways. There are really no definites, except the gradual slowing down of your mind and body. Your evolution is more in your control than you care to admit. You *can* evolve as the person you would like to be, as the partner you would like to have, as the human being you must live with for a long, long, long time. C. S. Lewis touched on this in his book *Mere Christianity* (Macmillan, New York: 1943). These aren't his words, but what he was driving at was that if we believe we are here today and gone tomorrow, we can behave as badly as we dare. But if we have any sense of eternity, the thought of living with "us"—not for eighty, but eight hundred or eight thousand or eight million years—will bring us up very short and force us to look very hard in the mirror *and* make the necessary changes!

THE PRIVATE SIDES OF
A MARRIAGE
PARTNERSHIP

INTIMACY

One of the greatest gaps between men and women is in their notion of what is emotional intimacy and how important they feel it is in a marriage.

—DANIEL GOLEMAN
(The New York Times)

*I*ntimacy doesn't come naturally. You have to learn it, accept it, give it, understand it. What makes it so difficult is that it takes time and experience and even some false starts to begin to understand its wonders and its depth of meaning. Some people learn intimacy at an early age. I didn't. But when I finally did I came to realize that I had to connect with another human being on a level that made every other relationship pale by comparison. Believe me when I say intimacy is the ultimate sharing, the really incredible side of love.

As I began to write this chapter my wife brought a small vase of roses into my office without saying a word. She's never done that before, nor did she know I was writing about intimacy. But what she did and how she did it and why she did it was an intimate act! Intimacy is far more, far deeper, and far less sexual than the word might imply. Intimacy is probably the single most important cornerstone/connection within a deep and lively love. Defining it is nearly impossible. Living it—in and out of each and every day—is really the only way of discovering its deeps, its importance, its centrality to a successful marital partnership.

Intimacy, particularly as it pertains to marriage, consists in my opinion of two parts:

1. loving your partner enough *and* yourself enough to let him or her into your private world, where all your feelings are gathered and to be able and willing to share those feelings without fear of judgment, rejection, *or* retribution.
2. loving yourself enough, *and* your partner enough, to be open and sensitive to what they carry in their hearts as well as in their minds.

IT DOESN'T JUST HAPPEN

It sounds so plausible and it is possible, but intimacy doesn't just happen. To quote Daniel Goleman in a *New York Times* article from 1986, part of the dilemma is the difference between males and females.

One of the great gaps between husbands and wives is in their notions of emotional intimacy and how important they feel it is in a marriage. For many men, simply doing such things as working in the garden or going to a movie with their wives gives them a feeling of closeness. But for their wives that is not enough, according to Ted Huston, a psychologist at the University of Texas at Austin who has studied 130 couples intensively. "For the wives, intimacy means talking things over, especially talking about the relationship itself," Dr. Huston said. "The men, by and large, don't understand what the wives want from them. They say, 'I want to do things with her, and all she wants to do is talk.' "

Men do have a harder time "opening up." Men don't cry as easily. Men think that "macho" is what is expected of them. Men tend to bottle up or "control" their feelings. Men are very often little boys in grown-up bodies, whose fears of rejection and being misunderstood cause them to act in ways that push away those who love and like them the most!

Women talk much more eagerly and easily about intimate things. Women will show and share their emotions/feelings, sometimes without any "controls," which can push away those who love and like them the most. Women demand intimacy, or at least sense its importance. Men shy away from it, and this is evidenced by the fact that men have far fewer "close friends" than do women.

Genetic differences accepted, both women and men in marriage partnerships *can* learn new and more intimate ways as they talk, work, play, listen, and love together.

SOME GUIDELINES FOR MEN

I think it's much harder for men to be intimate—at least that has been my observation and experience. Maybe what follows will help loosen you up.

1. Relax. It is okay to think and talk about your fears, your phobias, your likes, your dislikes, your job, your spouse, your family, your marriage.
2. Be direct.
3. Cry.
4. Don't hide behind anything or anybody. Your feelings are yours alone. Therefore they are very important to you. Let them out, if you dare and if you can.
5. Remember that there are no right or wrong feelings.
   It is sort of like going down a long stairway. There is light, so we can see, but it is what we might find out about ourselves and others that makes us hesitate. Don't! The journey is well worth the anxiety. The place you eventually find yourself in is better.
6. Trust yourself and your partner as if your life depended on it, which, in the sense of an intimate relationship, it does!

SOME GUIDELINES FOR WOMEN

It may be unfair to have a like number of guidelines for women, for you are way ahead of us males in this department, but these may help you look at your own defenses as well.

1. Focus your feelings by sorting out the immediate and important from all the others.
2. Face up to your feelings and frame them in such a way

that, when you present them, they make your partner part of the solution, not just one of the problems.

3. Be direct.
4. Be fair and be firm. Let your partner know what you like and dislike.
5. Don't rely on manipulation. You are intuitively very smart, so use those smarts to help your partner grow up and both of you to grow into the kind of relationship you want for the long pull.
6. Understand him. Allow him to please you and continue to court you, for therein he may be the most sensitive and open. Respect his maleness and your femininity, and rejoice in the difference!

SEXUAL INTIMACY

Although not the most important facet in or of an intimate relationship, the very word "intimate" has largely sexual connotations.

Sex is an intimate act, but true intimacy grows more out of what sex means to a couple, individually and together, than what they actually do in bed. Sexual intimacy is holding, snuggling, touching, and literally becoming connected with another human being. Pleasing and being pleasured are wonderful basic and physical experiences. Orgasms are mind-boggling and wonderful, even more so when people enjoy them together. But it is the closeness, the warmth of body and of mind, the inexplicable sense of oneness, the joy that such intimacy can bring—these are what truly being intimate is all about in the best sense of that word.

"Marriage is the only war in which you sleep with the enemy." [Unknown, "The Third Best Things Anybody Ever Said," Robert Byrne, Atheneum, New York, 1986.] Think about what that says. Sleeping with somebody you are mad at means feelings are acknowledged, dealt with, and tempered. Marriage can be a tug of war, and often, talking over tough things late into the night, in someone's arms, can begin the process of healing.

PHYSICAL INTIMACY

Physical intimacy can also be very sexual, but it is far more than that. Sitting in the same room with someone you love without touching or talking, but experiencing a deep sense of closeness, is physical intimacy. Being on a business trip and feeling the presence of your spouse a thousand miles away is physical intimacy. That feeling of oneness with you—the sharing of values and hopes and concerns and joys—while at the same time recognizing and reaffirming your separateness, your individuality, and the solitary that is within both of you, is physical intimacy. This is complicated and tricky, for it seems a contradiction. But think about it. How can you get close to him if you are not at home in your own heart? How can he sense who and where and what you are, if he is not anchored himself, by himself, in himself.

INTELLECTUAL INTIMACY

This is the sharing of ideas and plans and dreams. We get it all backward when we assume that people—couples, marriage partners—must agree. Maybe they will. Maybe they won't. It is that truly "intimate" connection born of intellectual exploration, discussion, argument, and consensus that enriches and enobles a marriage and the minds of those involved in it. One of the reasons you choose someone is because they "turn you on." You are turned on by people who fascinate you, challenge you, stretch your imagination, as well as your patience at times. You are turned on by unique, different, intriguing human beings and the ways they differ from you.

My wife and I have some hairy discussions, particularly on politics but:

1. We respect each other.
2. We recognize that we are both well-informed.
3. We are both opinionated *and* vocal.
4. We *try* to listen to each other's rantings and ravings.
5. We love each other enough to know that we do raise each other's consciousness and that that intrinsically is a good thing.

Respect, good ears, the willingness to change one's mind if persuaded, the grace to appreciate the health of different opinions, a love that is grounded enough to take some wear and strain—these are the ingredients for intellectual intimacy.

EMOTIONAL INTIMACY

The key to a healthy and deep relationship is emotional intimacy. Without it, sex, smarts, and closeness pale. To be in tune with another emotionally is the main symphony; the others are but "movements" of the whole. Marriage formally begins a life-long process within which two people—*if they choose*—can explore depths in their own and their partner's lives that they never knew existed. Many fear to open those doors, but no tigers lurk there. Behind each face and beneath each façade is a wonderfully complex and complete human being, who needs (not always wants) to learn the necessary skills and the temporary risks and the long-term joys of an emotionally intimate relationship. A surface intimacy may come in a short time, but a multilayered trusting and sharing, hearing and helping, growing and loving partnership is where a deep and lively love can lead you over the long pull.

You may be thinking, "Why can't I have that intimacy?" It is probably that very feeling of "I can't" that holds you back. Try the following exercise.

EXERCISE 7
Why Can't I?

For each of the following questions, ask yourself "Why can't I . . .

1. . . . encourage my partner to share what is on his or her mind and heart without censorship or muted feelings or proper language?

2. . . . realize that what I will hear will be their feelings—*not* necessarily the facts?

3. . . . admit there are no right or wrong feelings, and that any judgment on my part is not appropriate!?

4. . . . listen with compassion and concern *and* admiration for his or her willingness to talk?

5. . . . bite my tongue—and not confront or comment—and try to identify with his or her hurts or joys?

6. . . . think hard about what he or she is saying about *them?* Nine times out of ten he or she is *not* talking, much less thinking about me.

7. . . . reach out to him or her—physiologically and psychologically—with understanding, love, *and* good judgment?

8. . . . offer a suggestion, a hug, a diversion, a hand, a kiss?

Now go back, read each one out loud and answer, "I can," because, in fact, you can.

Whatever the cost, strive for the most intimate relationship possible, for therein lies the bedrock of a good marriage and the deepest understanding of love. Saint Paul's description of love in his remarkable letter to the Church at Corinth puts it in a marvelous frame.

"Love is patient; love is kind and envies no one. Love is never boastful, nor conceited, nor rude; never selfish, not quick to take offense. Love keeps no score of wrongs; does not gloat over other men's sins but delights in the truth. There is nothing love cannot face; there is no limit to its faith, its hope, and its endurance."

For a scrappy old bachelor who looked somewhat askance at marriage, Saint Paul has described intimacy—an intimate love—as well as I have ever heard it defined by anyone. In less logical terms, here is my working definition of intimacy: *Intimacy* is that extraordinary relational state in which *both* partners are finally able to respect and understand their own uniqueness and trust their chosen partners enough to share deep feelings (from joy to anger) and express deep love in conventional ways (listening, holding, forgiving) and in unconventional ways (crying, learning, *and* changing).

Be caring. Be close. Be aware of "the other" in you and your partner. Let yourself go—into their loving arms. Let yourself be vulnerable, for only thus will you experience intimacy. Finally, let yourself be yourself, for it is that true glimpse of you that allows me to like you and love you more than either one of us thought possible!

SEXUALITY

Love is not the dying moan of a distant violin—it's the triumphant twang of a bedspring.

—S. J. PERELMAN

Sex is important, fun, satisfying, creative, procreative, complicated, and extraordinarily powerful. Dealing with your own inherent sexuality and the quite different sexuality of your marriage partner is high on the list of things you *must* think about, talk about, and negotiate about, almost on a daily basis. Sex has made marriages and destroyed them. Sex has driven people into the arms of bliss and driven them to distraction. Sex and its inevitable fantasies can do some incredibly bad things to good judgment and good taste, and can do some incredibly wonderful things to those who rejoice in its mystery, its integrity, and its healthy drives.

IT'S DIFFICULT TO TALK ABOUT

We are still recovering from the sexual repression of the last century and the sexual revolution of this one! Sexuality remains constant, because basically people don't change, even though times do. Whether underground or above ground, the same sexual confusion and pressures seem to intrigue, haunt, and often hinder the free and responsible exercise of our sexuality.

Part of the problem, at least from my experience as a parish priest and counselor, is that sex is extraordinarily difficult to talk about. We will make jokes about it, but we can't seem to deal with it as directly as we do with our need for shelter or food or warmth. It is just as basic—in fact, we probably think about it more—"but our lips are sealed."

I will never forget attending a conference on human sexuality in the late sixties and hearing the speaker use a four-letter word in a public address. It was done gracefully and for a reason. It freed her listeners to the use of language—basic sexual language—to help talk directly about sexual desires, sexual needs, and sexual facts. If partners in a marriage would be a little less polite and evasive and more explicit and direct in talking about their sexuality, I am convinced that a lot of assumptions and hangups could come tumbling down! There is only a bit of difference between the statements "I like you" and "You turn me on," but the difference in meaning is enormous. Words are the only direct connection we have to our emotions, because body language is harder to interpret. I urge you all, particularly in this crucial area, to be up front with your feelings and the words you use to make them known.

SEX IS IMPORTANT

Sex is important to your state of mind and your state of health. Individuals vary in their sexual interests and habits, but we are all sexual beings. We all lust. We all seek sexual pleasure either through the body of another or by our own hand. Animalistic or not, it is the way we are made. How you accept this natural state and how you respect its natural boundaries says volumes about how complete you feel you are. Because sex is so important, you must understand its positives and its negatives. For example, using another human being purely for sexual release, without regard for his or her feelings, is a form of rape. You have to be responsible for your own sexual acts. You have to set limits. You must care for and respect the other person and yourself as well. Promiscuous sexual behavior demeans, destroys, and dehumanizes everyone involved.

On the positive side, people who rejoice in their own sexuality and allow themselves to express and experience sex in healthy and monogamous ways with partners who truly excite them and expand their horizons are more in touch with the meaning and importance of sex.

SEX IS FUN

Sex is fun and sex is also funny, when you think of all the flirting, fussing, deception, undressing, contortions, posturing, positioning, groaning, and moaning we go through to achieve the apex of sexual experience—"the orgasm."

Sex is fun, because it involves or should involve play. There is a wonderful playfulness that can go along with sexual exploration that helps keep it youthful, slightly irreverent, and more than slightly fascinating. Fun is a key ingredient in healthy sexual interaction, and laughter at its joys and its silliness keeps it anchored and free. Take sex seriously, but have fun while thinking about it, talking about it, and while trying to perform those acrobatic feats that the sex manuals suggest!

SEX IS SATISFYING

Sex is satisfying and it should be! Contrary to the British mother's advice on her daughter's wedding night ("close your eyes and think of England") sex can be one of the most deeply satisfying experiences you are privileged to enjoy as human beings and there are at least four good reasons why:

1. It feels good. In fact, it feels terrific! The arousal and climax in sexual intercourse is a human experience unequaled and indescribable!
2. It feels good all over, from the tips of your toes to the top of your head. To love and be loved, to hold and be held, to touch and be touched, to arouse and be aroused, to enter another's body or receive another's body into ours, com-

mingling in eventual orgasm, makes you tremble and shiver and feel incredible all over—physically and mentally.

3. Sexual activity makes you feel more complete—as man and as woman and as a couple—for it is so much a part of your psyche that its expression, being acted out as well as enjoyed, is satisfying to your ego.

4. A balanced and regular and creative sexual relationship can give you satisfaction as deep as you could hope for.

HAVE CREATIVE SEX

Sex must be creative. Ovid once wrote, "Skill makes love unending," and it does help! Sex may be a natural function, but that doesn't mean it is automatically terrific. Preferences, expectations, and techniques need to be addressed. I believe that whatever a couple *decides* is okay for them is okay—that is short of "S and M" or group sex, which I think are *bad* news.

Everyone has preferences, largely unstated, but they need to be discussed. If I can ask you on these pages whether you prefer oral sex or mutual masturbation or rear entry or the missionary position or sideways or underneath or on top or whatever, you can certainly ask your marriage partner these questions in the privacy of your own bedroom! People like different things. People have different fantasies. People have different hangups. Share them, hear and respect your partner's feelings, take what you have learned and agreed on, and then enjoy each other more in bed.

Important, too, are your mutual expectations regarding frequency, orgasms, foreplay, and the like. Sex is too important to guess about, and it is a whole lot better to say exactly what we expect. You will feel less guilty about not wanting to have sex, you will feel less badly about "being rejected," if you have been living in an atmosphere of expressed expectations.

To think about techniques may sound a bit mechanical, but they are important. Careless, untutored, insensitive sexual behavior is no less a turn-off than having your finger slammed in a door. Gentleness, awareness of the parts of your partner's body that are particularly sensitive, patience, the willingness to peruse good sexual manuals are a sign of a caring, mature lover who wants to please his or her partner by becoming better at making love.

SEX IS PROCREATIVE

The creation of children by you—the procreators—is the greatest privilege, opportunity, and responsibility you are given as human beings.

Babies conceived by teenagers out of wedlock, babies conceived by a couple who are not emotionally ready to be parents, babies conceived by people who then care more about their unborn fetus than their eventual unwanted child, babies conceived by men and women who scoff at contraception—these babies are denied the life, the freedom, the opportunity, irresponsible conceivers take for granted. That's not fair!

Procreative sex must be separated from recreational sex, so that when partners choose to conceive a child, they know exactly what they are doing!

SEX IS COMPLICATED

Sex mirrors so closely your own very complicated mood swings, feelings, phobias, your intricate mental and physical balances. Sex is far more in the mind than in the genitals. Impotence is usually a psychological rather than a physiological malady. You cannot separate your sexuality from the rest of life. It is all connected and it is all very complicated. That is why inappropriate sexual behavior always comes home to haunt us. If simple masturbation, which has its place and can be a healthy release, can make you feel guilty, you see what more bizarre practices can do to your head. Sex is not to be toyed with, literally and figuratively.

Sex is powerful! Havelock Ellis (1859–1939) in *The New Spirit* wrote, "The omnipresent process of sex, as it is woven into the whole texture of our man's or woman's body, is the pattern of all the process of our life." Its universality and its power over individual lives is almost immeasurable as any cursory reading of ancient or modern history will testify. Sex is incredibly powerful, and you need to admit that and deal with it before you become its slave. People use their sexuality in so many complicated ways for so many complicated reasons. You should be aware that sex can reflect rage (as in rape), anger (as in adultery), sickness (as in incest), selfishness (as in promiscuous messing around). It can also reflect your most powerful and positive feelings for another human being in a most powerful and positive way. Sexual union between two committed, caring, consenting adults is probably the most powerful force that can be unleashed any place, any time, by any two people. Treat it and its subjects with enormous respect and care."

GOOD, HEALTHY SEX

Here are four quite disparate, but I think important, observations as we look at our sexual proclivities. What follows deals with our overall sexual health and how we must be sensitive to that fine line between what helps and what hinders us as we act out our desires.

1. Fantasy can be a helpful tool in enriching sexual enjoyment, as long as it does not become the primary focus. Erotic thoughts, underwear, books, and films can be very arousing, but they are a means to an end and not the end in itself. Materials like this can also become addictive, so they must be used sparingly and wisely. Fantasy can help us over low periods—periods of wavering interest, which can happen to the best of us—but only as an aphrodisiac. Fantasy can create the proper mood, help rekindle tired feelings, and even facilitate orgasm, but we must "fall

again" for our real partners and fall into their arms with new excitement and commitment.

2. Don't use sex as a weapon! It will only come back to haunt you later on. There are better ways to fight and punish.

3. Sexual urges can delude us into mistaking lust for love. Sex is the great deluder, as you can see by the sordid tales and affairs and marital failures that fill the history books and daily news. You would think people would learn from experience, but we tend not to.

4. Masturbation is a natural release and is *not* instinctively bad. Director Milos Forman once said, "What I like about masturbation is that you don't have to talk afterward." It is a silly observation, but strangely enough, it is also to the point, because solitary sex is not where one finds deep satisfaction or "the coupling" that joint sexual experience brings. Masturbation is a better choice than adultery, but not comparable to the joys and pleasures of having and holding another person in sexual union and love.

Rejoice in your sexuality. Be responsive and responsible as you act and live it out with your partner in love. Treat it and them with respect and with wonder, for sexual joy can be the ultimate and intimate bonding between you!

FIDELITY

*No matter how happily a woman may be
married, it always pleases her to discover
that there is a nice man who wishes she
were not.*

—H. L. MENCKEN

I dare say that the Eleventh
Commandment ought to be "Thou shalt not mess around!"
Fidelity has to do with trust, and once trust is broken, it can
take a long, long time—if ever—to reestablish. Marital fidelity
is on a different plane from other forms of trust. Business
trust, if broken, can usually be repaired without long-term
recriminations. Public trust, if broken by a candidate, may be
eventually overlooked. But the inherent trust between two
human beings, two marriage partners, two people whose
commitment is based largely on confidence in the other's
integrity, is truly unique. Mess with it or "mess around" and
you have a real mess on your hands, for the very core of what

we call "honor" is directly wired to the promise of love and security our partner guarantees.

PAUSE, PRAY, AND DON'T PLAY AROUND

Affairs are as old as history and, as someone once remarked, "There is no such thing as original sin. It is all very unoriginal." Cheating on one's wife or husband has been going on for thousands of years, but that doesn't mean it is a good idea! In fact, it is a lousy idea, for an affair affects not just you and your paramour, but your spouses, your marriages, and often your children and your friends as well. Affairs erode your home life, your integrity, and your judgment. The latter usually goes first, because it is usually bad judgment that leads us down the garden path in the first place.

I'm not denying that marriage partners can lose interest in each other or that relationships moderate or that attraction can wane or that love can turn sour. All these are possible and even probable if partners don't constantly "retune" their relationships. What I am saying is that having an affair turns one problem into at least two! Look at the problems that fuel affairs and see what alternate corrective measures might have been taken. Maybe nothing will work and the marriage should die. But it behooves you to try to preserve the trust and the dignity inherent in your relationship by first handling the issues rather than another human being! In other words, pause and pray and *don't* play around. Think—and don't shrink—from the facts.

FIRST COMES LONELINESS

Sex is usually part of an affair *but* it follows, rather than precedes, the "involvement." This is important to keep in mind, because more often than not, loneliness rather than lust starts the ball rolling. Here are two very common examples.

The husband feels alone and unable to talk with his wife about his job, his boss, his fears at work, his frustrations at home. So he talks to his secretary, who sees him for more waking hours than his wife does and who knows him almost as well. Or he sees another manager, who happens to be female, or even an old girlfriend. She listens and she is "interested," or at least he perceives it that way. So he talks more and she listens more, they begin to have lunch together and call each other; eventually they arrange a "business meeting," which usually ends up in bed!

A wife whose children are now all in school and has gone back to work herself finds new challenges, fascinating people, and an atmosphere that seems less humdrum and more exciting than home. Male co-workers seem to find her attractive, and she finds she dresses for them rather than for her husband. They treat her as an equal, as a beautiful woman, and someone who is important in her own right. Like the example before, she is drawn slowly but surely into a new relationship that at first parallels her marriage. Then, because of its excitement and newness, it eclipses her marriage emotionally and eventually sexually.

IT CAN HAPPEN TO YOU

We are all human and we all have similar needs, particularly in the arena of marital commitment and the expectations such a relationship breeds. If you feel, rightly or wrongly, that your needs are not being met at home, you are more vulnerable and ripe for extracurricular activity. A word to the wise and the unwise! *It can happen to you. It can happen to your spouse.* Affairs can mess up your head and your marriage. We must be careful and alert to situations that can literally drive your partner into another's arms! Following are four "do nots" that should help you stay on track:

1. Do not take your partner for granted. You should look at your partner—*daily*—with new eyes and fresh appreciation. If he or she and you, for that matter, feel appreciated at home, there won't be a need for seeking reaffirmation elsewhere. We all need others to interact with professionally and good friends to interact with socially. In fact, good friends are a special buffer and a sounding board that can greatly enrich and cement a marriage. But if we feel like a full partner at home, we won't be inclined to seek marital strokes someplace else.

2. Do not be excessively jealous. Believe it or not, an overtly jealous spouse can literally drive his or her mate into doing the very thing they fear the most—having an affair! Be attentive. Be concerned. Be protective. Speak out loud and clear, if someone makes a move on your spouse. But *don't* smother with jealous accusations or try to restrict your spouse's movements. They may start to fulfill your prophecy.

3. Do not encourage inappropriate, intimate relationships. Boundaries and responsibility and ethical behavior are key concepts here. It is unfair and unwise and unhealthy to take advantage of a parishioner or a patient or an employee or anyone who looks to you for solace or sustenance. Do

not fool around with another's head or body. Do not feed dangerous fantasies.

I know of cases where a doctor slept with a patient, a clergyman seduced a damaged parishioner, a boss took a young secretary to a convention as his wife. They were wrong. But also wrong are fathers who treat their daughters as their sweethearts and mothers who try to make a son into a substitute husband.

4. Do not think the grass is greener in the neighbor's yard. It isn't, nor is the "neighbor" the answer to our prayer! The person we decide to have a fling with is usually more or as screwed up, literally and figuratively, as we are. Besides which, two wrongs do not make a right, and no good can come of it.

When we feel an inappropriate attraction coming on, we need to face up to it and deal with it. A counselor I know suggested that if you find you are literally "possessed" by another person, you should "act out the affair" in your head—in total detail. When I first heard this, I thought he was crazy. But I think it works. By giving yourself permission to do in your mind what you are thinking about doing in person, you force yourself to deal with the realities as well as the romantic notions that consume you. The "afterward" can look pretty grim, therefore providing you with a preview of how you might feel or what you might find if you actually "consummated the affairs."

Are there any other reasons we shouldn't sleep around? As if the safety of your partnership were not enough, what I heard on a CBS documentary on AIDS answers the question better than I can: When you have sex with someone, you not only have sex with them, but with everyone they have had sex with for the last five to seven years.

SET BEHAVIORAL LIMITS

Behavior—your behavior and your partner's reaction to your behavior—sets certain boundaries that help "keep you in the yard," so to speak. Let me use a huge generalization to make this point. Women tend to be more masochistic than men. They seem to put up with questionable behavior, they'll not protest when their husbands come home very late or very drunk or when they "work" sixteen hours a day. Men tend to be more narcissistic or unaware than women, assuming that whatever they do, unless challenged, is okay. Men can be very obtuse and obstinate, which complicates the cycle, for their behavior, if not checked, feeds back into the masochistic syndrome, and nothing changes. Behavioral limits must be set, by both partners, or two individuals have simply passed in the night—and neither one is wiser.

A woman is at a party and some man pinches her fanny. If her husband sees it, but does or says nothing, what does that say to her? He doesn't care! If a man comes home late at night with a buzz on or lipstick on his cheek and his wife says nothing, what does that say to him? She doesn't care! It is out of this seeming indifference that new behavioral patterns are formed, and they are usually bad patterns—patterns that could lead you into extra-marital involvements at worst, or insular living at best.

FUNDS IN TRUST

Fidelity has other facets—less dramatic perhaps, but still crucial to the health of your partnership. How you trust your partner's handling of money or your investments can affect the way you feel about each other. The expression "trust me" simply isn't good enough. Deeds, performances, results are what count. Coming home when you say you will or calling if delayed, listening to concerns about a bill or about a person or an event, knowing that whatever happens your partner will be there—all these are the bedrock on which trust and fidelity stand.

THE PAST IS PAST

What has gone before should be left right there. Don't talk about past escapades with your marriage partner unless you have a marriage death wish. What is past is past and really has nothing to do with your present relationship. Look at it another way. How would you like your wife or your husband to list by number and name their former flames or lovers? It would destroy you and maybe your marriage as well. Leave the past where it belongs—forgotten and forgiven.

I'm for open marriage, but sometimes we can be open to such a degree that we "cleanse *our* soul" at someone else's expense by dumping the gory details and the guilt of what we have done on them. That is a stupid and mean thing to do. Show and tell may be just fine for kindergarten children, but it is a dangerous game for adults. Be sure of what you are sharing *and* why you are sharing it. Be very careful of the person you share it with. A woman in premarital counseling was urged by her intended to tell him everything she had done, and with whom, before they met. She refused. He asked again and again. She refused again and again. He begged her to tell him. Eventually, he wore her down and she told it all—and there was lots to tell! He was devastated and, as a result, so was she. He shouldn't have pressed her. She shouldn't have told him. This so-called "openness" almost cost them their marriage.

POSTSCRIPT

I want to add a postscript to this that has more to do with forgiveness than with fidelity, but you will see how they are connected. As I suggested, the Eleventh Commandment should be "Thou shalt not mess around." I mean just that and I underline the admonition a hundred times. *Don't do it!*

However, we *are* human and we can get ourselves into a jam, sometimes even before we know it. I'm not condoning inappropriate behavior, but I am cautioning you to look at the facts before slamming any doors. One-night stands are a bad idea and a bad mistake. But if it does happen we need to look at the cause as well as the effect. We need to measure one stupid act against a good, long-term marriage relationship. I'm not suggesting a whitewash or looking the other way or a "boys will be boys" attitude. I'm suggesting tough love—a clear setting forth of the damage done and the understanding that any repeat performance will not be tolerated. I'm also suggesting forgiveness—not forgetting, but forgiveness—so that the marriage partnership, if basically sound, can restart its engines.

FAMILY AND CHILDREN

A happy family is but an earlier heaven.
—SIR JOHN BOWRING

My *immediate* family—meaning my wife and myself, the nine children we have between us, the five in-laws, seven going on eight grandchildren—equals twenty-three people! Our *close* families—meaning our twenty-three, two remaining parents, eight siblings and their five spouses, twenty-two nieces and nephews plus their six mates and seven children, two aunts and one uncle—comes to seventy-six!!

The reason to extrapolate these numbers is to show how vast our families can be. These families can and do have a definite effect on our marital relationships. You may be individuals, but you are not alone, and the sooner you understand this matrix of outsiders who press in on your territory and try to influence your marriage, the better your chances for survival!

For example, my mother looks on her children's spouses as nice and necessary adjuncts to her children, but that's about all. They are not really central as "members of the family." My mother-in-law goes to the other extreme. Both women are thoughtful, wonderful people who are simply reflecting their—and possibly their parents' before them—manner of dealing with in-laws. To take offense or "take to the hills" would miss the point.

YOU MARRY A FAMILY

You each bring to the marriage partnership your history, your heritage, your particular and peculiar way of looking at and doing things. That composite is you. One way to understand and appreciate your mate and yourself is to check all this out before and during the marriage. You need to look at *all* the family members and family systems that impinge on your marriage, because they are part and parcel of "the partnership."

Why is it so surprising for the daughter of an alcoholic to be adamant against drinking, or in another case to drift toward alcoholism herself? Why shouldn't a man brought up by a single, strong, possessive woman, who lived vicariously through her son, seek out a woman to fill this continuing and unhealthy role as a wife? Victims of child abuse may be particularly vulnerable to even more abuse in their grown-up years. A permissive parent, whose permissiveness is in direct retaliation for his or her own strict upbringing, may mix up love and discipline so badly that the adored and spoiled child spins out of control and into deep trouble. The examples are many, but the simple message is to take a hard look at all the hands that are on your marriage, all the influences that mold it, and all the people whose views and practices and habits are inherent in your spouse and in you. To look is to see; to listen is to hear; to understand is to be able to learn and live with the "composite person."

Two people come together, commit to a partnership, and walk together into the tomorrows, but they do not travel alone! I was told years ago by my grandmother, "You marry a family." The old girl knew what she was talking about, for we do "marry" more than one. In fact, we inherit a group!

EXERCISE 8
Genograms

You need to draw a family map, chart, or what some call "genograms." On a sheet of paper put yourself and your spouse in the middle of the page, and then, branching out from you, your parents, siblings, aunts and uncles, grandparents. Include any children or stepchildren. By each name indicate with a word or two what comes into your mind when you think about them: tough, a drinker, sensitive, great fun, difficult, easygoing. Add their profession to give another dimension and if they are dead or alive, at home or wherever.

Now take a look at the players and realize how their backgrounds and behaviors and what they do for a living affects your own outlook on life and play and work *and* relationships! We carry into our new partnerships an established heritage, habits, inherited prejudices, and a very definite family identity. You need to understand that just as much as you need to understand yourself as a limb of another tree that you can't cut down or be cut away from. However, what you can do is look at where you came from and what's out there that could adversely impact your present relationship.

John Tyndall (1820–1893) wrote in Volume II of *Fragments of Science*, "We are truly heirs of all the ages; but as honest men it behooves us to learn the extent of our inheritance, and as brave ones not to whimper if it should prove less than we had supposed." We carry with us our true inheritance—good and bad—but it is improvable! That is why it is worth your while to draw your map and learn its lessons.

BE HONEST ABOUT YOUR FEELINGS

We are extraordinarily sensitive about the imperfections in our parents or siblings and especially in our children. We'll even deny or avoid talking about some obvious faults because they can be very threatening to our self image *and* our family image—the fantasy we chose as we were growing up.

A close friend of mine was brought up by important, successful, and well-liked parents. He was constantly being told how lucky he was to have such wonderful parents, which made it almost impossible for him to even look at, much less deal with, their imperfections. The truth is that they rarely spent much time with him or his sister, and such time that was made available was spent in adult rather than child activities. They were treated as little people, not as children. There were no real connections between him and his parents—no feelings shared, hugs, working together on projects, playing catch. But it wasn't until he was in therapy, years later, that he could admit that he was sad and mad about "not having parents" in the normal sense of that word; that they may have been marvelous human beings, but that they were less than adequate nurturers. That cleared the air for him, and it cleared up a mystery his wife had been trying to figure out ever since he had blown up about her parents calling them too frequently. He had been jealous and couldn't connect it or admit it.

It is hard to hear the truth about a member of your family from someone else's mouth. I'm not saying partners in a marriage don't need to do just that—particularly if the family attitude, activity, authority, or influence is negatively affecting the marriage—but be careful *and* be gentle. "It is okay for me to criticize my brother, but don't you do it!" is a somewhat typical response.

You need to learn new ways of looking at, and talking about, your family so you can see them more clearly and, in turn, see how they have influenced you. Sometime the clearest picture is shown to you by the one person who sees you and them from more of a distance; i.e., your own spouse! You need to lower your defenses, open your ears, hear what the facts are. Fantasy can only lead to deeper disappointments.

YOUR PARENTS AND YOUR CHILDREN

Regarding the immediate family, let me posit a thought that has helped me keep these tricky relationships in better balance over the years. It has to do with reality, acceptance, forgiveness, and understanding.

Parents by definition are perfect. Therefore, they can do no wrong, and hence, there is no need to forgive them. This is obviously not true, but it is where a lot of people get hung up and stay semiparalyzed *and* very angry. But parents are also people. People can do stupid and mean things, and need forgiveness and another chance. You need to try to look at your parents as people, for only then will you understand their parenting and be able to enjoy them as individuals and unique personalities.

The same is true with your children. Children, by definition, are your issue, your extension, your immortality, and hence, they should do no wrong. Your reaction to bad behavior is usually very oppressive *or* very permissive, with little in between. This too is crazy, for your children are not your clones. In fact, they only have half of your genes to begin with and, if you go back to your genogram, you will see how many other strands are also centered in them. They are individuals. They deserve to be allowed to grow up and develop as the unique people they are! Forgiveness, setting limits, trust and confidence in their inherent strengths will allow them to be people as well as your progeny.

Your parents are *people* first, your parents second. Your children are *people* first, your children second.

THE CHILDREN COME SECOND

Some people choose to live alone. People who get married choose to live with another, and by such action form a family, a unit, a partnership. Families start and are centered on the husband and the wife. That union comes first—at first and later. This is a key point. You fall in love, commit to and want to spend your life with another person—not persons! You, the couple, the partners, must be the number-one priority in the relationship. Children not only come later, but must come second in a relationship. This is easy to say before the fact, and a lot harder to practice afterward, but children are the result of a marriage, not the reason for it. Children come, grow up, and leave, leaving the parents where they started— alone together. If the parents' relationship has gotten lost in the confusion, in conflicts of bringing up children, their life together "after the kids leave" probably won't be so terrific. It is hard to rekindle a flame or be alone with a "stranger."

There are hundreds of books on bringing up children, so I won't be presumptuous and add more than my two cents. I do, however, suggest four parental actions that will help children of all ages act out and act on their better instincts:

1. Let children be children. Allow them to grow up gradually and not lose the spontaneity and foolishness and fun of childhood. Let them be themselves—not little people or dolls or clones.
2. Let children experiment. Allow them to pick up and poke at life as it unfolds before them. Set limits and stick to them, but help them discover their strengths and recognize their weaknesses.

3. Let children fail. Some parents are possessed by wanting their children to get all A's in school or get letters in sports or the best job with the best firm. Let them be themselves. That will include some failures, but out of the experiences will come wiser, stronger, nicer human beings.

4. Let children go. Don't hang on as they peek out the door and around the corner. They *will* leave you. They *must* leave you, and only if they do, will they be able to return as healthy adults. We need to wean our children before, not after, they start to walk.

CLARITY, BALANCE, AND BEHAVIOR

We are forever talking about family trees. How about focusing on family "shrubs"—your own little corners in the larger family forest? The husband and wife are the number-one priority. From this plateau of love and strength the family develops and family life is structured. *Clarity, balance*, and *behavior* are key words.

You should be very *clear* about what you want and why—from the number of children to how you would like them brought up. If you are clear with each other as partners and later on as partner/parents, you and your children will have an easier and better time growing up—a process not exclusively the realm of our offspring! Clarity about where you want to live and why; clarity about the kind of neighborhood, house, school, and friends you see; clarity about who does what around the apartment or the house; clarity about expected time together, joint activities. Clarity—directness—is a must, if couples and, in turn, their families are to communicate effectively and efficiently.

Balance is also important, and it is so easy to get out of balance as the politeness of courtship gives way to the harsher mechanics of life together as a family. Balance is essential; balance between time spent at and away from home; balance between work and play; balance between spouse and children; balance between whatever you enjoy the most and need to do the most. Balanced people are collected people, and because of that, there is a rhythm to their lives that is engaging and enhancing.

Behavior is the great leveler, for it not only directly affects a family and its complicated relationships, but it also sends long and loud signals to those you love the most, but sometimes treat the worst. You are responsible for your behavior—not anyone else's. Your example can have a huge impact on how your partner and your children act and react. You do not live in a vacuum. Deeds speak louder than words. Your behavior is what tells the real story about how much you care for yourself and about other people. Don't act out or act up without taking a long and careful look in the mirror and then into the next room as well.

As Sir John Bowring so beautifully said, "A happy family is but an earlier heaven." From this happy family emerges our children. You can do much to insure that from within and then out from your family shrubs will emerge individuals who possess a healthy sense of love, a deep feeling of caring and of being cared for, and a real purpose and a plan for living.

REMARRIAGE AND STEPCHILDREN

When a woman marries again, it is because she detested her first husband. When a man marries again, it is because he adored his first wife.

—OSCAR WILDE
(The Picture of Dorian Gray)

*M*arriage relationships can flounder, love can die, partnerships sometimes will not work any longer, despite intense counseling and time spent working on them.

There is nothing sadder, except maybe the death of a spouse, than to see a marriage, a couple, a family fall away and fall apart. It is devastating, difficult, and it takes a long, long time to recover. Love and hate are the reverse sides of the same coin and this becomes painfully clear when lovers turn into enemies before our very eyes. Divorce is never "best," particularly when there are children. It can be the "better" choice, however, if two individuals are so dramatically out of sync that what once was is no longer and their journey together has become a journey of pain, rather than one of joy.

DIVORCE AND DESPAIR

What drives people to divorce is usually despair. The loneliness and confusion inherent in that state of mind often first drive them into someone else's arms. People who leave home for someone else are leaving home for the wrong reasons. The "other person" may well be a catalyst, but the state of the marriage itself, the feelings or lack of feelings for the present marriage partner, these "at-home factors" are generally the reason behind any considered change.

This is not a book about divorce or despair, so I'll leave those subjects to the mediators and counselors and authors who deal with this huge and sad phenomenon on a far more professional basis. However, people who do go through divorce and its despair for good and bad reasons often want to get remarried and this usually involves a step-family.

REMARRIAGE IS A TALL ORDER!

All the things we talked about in the past eleven chapters hold true for second marriages as well. But remarried people have to recognize that they bring to the new partnership, in addition to everything else, some bulky baggage:

1. Unfinished business with a former spouse, be it financial, personal, or emotional.

2. Personal emotional baggage, such as guilt and feelings of failure.
3. Economic pressures.
4. Step-children.

Let me make an observation that I believe to be true, based on my own experience and what I have heard and observed as a counselor and priest for the last twenty years. *For a second marriage to work, counseling is essential!* There are too many variables, unknowns, and booby traps out there not to hire a guide to help you through the swamps and the jungle. My wife and I went for counseling before and after our wedding, and I am convinced that we couldn't have made it without it. In fact, it was the best wedding present we could have received.

UNFINISHED BUSINESS

When you leave one job or city for another, there are inevitably things you fail to deal with. Either you put them off or you simply have too much to do in too brief a period of time. Leaving a marriage is basically no different. There are some far tougher issues you don't want to face at all, because they are very, very painful. For a new marriage to work, however, the personal memories and personal effects of the old must be dealt with or the residue will carry over, with ill winds, into the new marriage.

Failure to really separate is a dangerous trap. Maintaining an ongoing relationship with a former spouse divides your attention and energy. It is often a hostile act, although you may not want to admit that. In any case, it prevents you from closing one chapter and properly starting another.

A specific example comes to mind. A man I know left his wife and claimed he wanted a divorce. This came after months of counseling together and alone. He moved out, but he called her almost daily, took her out for dinner, and even went back for some weekends. He felt he was being "nice," when in fact, it was nasty, for it kept her, who didn't want the separation in the first place, in emotional limbo. Now he is moving toward the divorce, but any future partner had better make darn sure he has really finished his business with his former wife before she signs on.

Another example of this has to do with property. I've seen divorced people sharing their old summer cottage or holding back on a piece of furniture "for the sake of the children" when, in fact, neither one would give up *their* stake. Hence, another piece of unfinished business that keeps them connected. I'm not suggesting that former spouses can't be friends and shouldn't be, but even that can only happen when the unfinished business is resolved. Everything improves for everyone when you finally separate. Wounds can heal. New life can begin. Remarriage then has a chance.

THAT EXCESS BAGGAGE

A person just doesn't walk out of one deep personal relationship, however painful, and into another, however blissful, without bringing along a lot of residual emotions, feelings of guilt and/or of abandonment, old habits, and personal quirks. Before even thinking about remarriage, you should do your best to unpack, sort out, and discard what is no longer useful or important. Emotions need to be sorted out. A feeling of anger coupled with a sense of loss and even some residual love for your ex-partner is natural. Admit it. Look at it. Understand it. Deal with it. Then move on. Feelings handled head-on are more easily coped with. To admit feeling angry, cheated, abandoned, or just plain lonely can be the beginning of some real healing!

Guilt is a monster! We all have it. We all feel it. We all hate to admit it. The good news is that you can work your way through your guilt *if* you give it your attention, your time, and the opportunity of feeling forgiven—primarily by yourself! You *should* feel like hell when you leave your spouse. You *should* feel terribly about not being a live-in parent or the one remaining parent. You *should* feel guilty about being "the survivor" either of a divorce or a death. It is what we *do* with these feelings that can make the difference between becoming a new person or a person who is "stuck."

Therapy is undoubtedly the best answer. Working through these emotions is the best way I know of accepting reality and yourself *and* the new responsibilities resulting from a death or a divorce. Remarriage takes all your energy, and there is little to spare for a guilt that is grounded in the past, rather than the present relationship. Work it through and work it out, before saying "I do" to anyone new!

Habits and personal quirks may require major surgery. You probably know way down deep what irritates those close to you.

The next exercise may seem a bit strange and even silly, but I think it is important to do.

EXERCISE 9
Examine Yourself

1. Strip naked, mentally and physically, and stand in front of a full-length mirror for five minutes.
2. It will seem like an eternity, but look hard in that mirror.
3. Ask yourself what you see.
4. Look again!!
5. If you were someone else, what would you like to see changed in yourself and in your behavior?

You have "seen" yourself without any of those coverings you normally hide behind and, believe it or not, others see you more honestly than you see yourself. That is an impetus to do something about yourself—in fact, pretend you had to walk out of your room into the living room. What would you have to change to have your family see and like the real you??

THOSE MONEY PRESSURES

Money pressures almost always dramatically increase when a divorce takes place, regardless of whether you are the one who left or the one who was left. Two people living apart cannot live as cheaply as two people living together. Add another person or persons and it gets a lot more expensive! People getting remarried need to get their pencils out *before* the wedding. Money pressures wreak havoc if they are not resolved. Assumptions about money—how much you have, how little you have—are usually inaccurate and erroneous. Be realistic and don't pretend all is well if it isn't. Surprises about money are a lot worse than facing up to the way it was and is going to be. It is what you don't know and then find out that can literally blow up a second marriage.

THE STEPCHILDREN

The issue of stepchildren is in a league all by itself. Stepparenting can be taxing, depressing, and debilitating. Stepchildren can also be wonderful, and stepparenting very rewarding, but it takes a lot of patience, wisdom, negotiating, and understanding on everyone's part to make it work.

Stepfamilies are *not* "The Brady Bunch"! Stepchildren are in a lot of emotional and personal confusion, especially at first. Recognizing the realities, accepting the fact that making a stepfamily work requires an enormous amount of effort and love, is the first hurdle.

It is impossible to deal in these few paragraphs with the problems and the possibilities of stepfamilies. What follows are some observations I've made based on my own experience and that of people I've worked with. (There is also a raft of good material by the Vishers and others on this mid-twentieth-century phenomenon (How to Win as a Step Family, Emily and John Visher, Dembner Books (Norton) New York: 1982). Reread "Hansel and Gretel" and Cinderella" and remember that the children were nursed on these stories. They might be harboring some hidden fears and doubts.)

1. Treat stepchildren initially like visitors from another country who, because of some "conflict over there," have been forced to live with you for a period of time. This recognizes their pain and your uncertainty. It takes time to get used to a new place and new players.

2. Run the household as it always has been run, including enforcing "house rules." These may differ from the rules they are used to, but all children, stepchildren in particular, need order, consistency, and limits. Don't be seduced by the erroneous thought that, if you give in, they will love you more. They won't. It wouldn't work with your own children, so why should it be different with your stepchildren?

3. Accept and reinforce their allegiance and love for their biological parent who is absent. You cannot compete with your counterpart (whether dead or distant), nor should you try.

4. Treat them as children, but not as "your" children. You are their parent's spouse. You live in the same house. You are an adult and an authority figure, such as a teacher might be. You can become their special friend, but this takes time and cannot be forced.

5. Watch out for manipulation, at which *all* young people are masters. You and your new spouse need to stand

together and not be "divided and conquered." Natural parents are exposed to this, but second-marriage parents get it in spades. Work out your differences in private, your public stance is a united front. Everyone wins if everyone knows parents speak with *one* voice.

6. Watch out for "stepparent fatigue," which can literally lay you low. Stepparenting is a tough job and its rewards are often unclear. You need to be empathetic toward your partner and yourself. Time alone and away to recharge and refocus is a must. Questions such as "How did I ever get myself into this?" need to be vented, even if not answered!

7. Spend time alone with your *own* children. You should do it in any case, but especially in remarriage situations. Children of all ages crave the attention and time of their parents together and alone; particularly, the latter, as they grow up and grow older.

8. Look on stepchildren as adjunct members of the family, almost like in-laws. Welcome them into the fold. Do not call a stepdaughter "my daughter" or go to the other extreme by referring to a stepson as "him." They *are* part of you now *and a very special part*. They have a lot to deal with—the new status of their parents, then their own identity, then their new and extended family. Don't mess it and them up by trying to fulfill your own emotional needs at their expense.

9. Be sensitive to the fact that stepchildren have two homes as well as different customs and traditions. Be aware that they may be worried about who will support them financially and who will get Dad's or Mom's money. Like all kids, they have divided loyalties and, at times, conflicting

emotions about a lot of things, including their stepparents. Tell your children and stepchildren that in remarried families members are not replaced—new members come in!

10. Above all, be yourself. When you are angry, you should show it appropriately, but with vigor. When you are pleased, you should express it, specifically, and with praise and thanks.

Stepchildren and stepparents are fellow human beings and it is that inherent humanity, with all its dimensions and expressions, that must be allowed to surface.

IT CAN WORK

Let me end this chapter with an assurance born out of a lot of personal and professional experience that both remarriage and stepparenting *can* work and can work well, if you put as much into them as you expect to get out of them. This sounds so trite, but it is so true.

Any worthwhile relationship has a cost, and that cost is a combination of patience, understanding, forgiveness, *and* permission to live and let live.

We recently had a family wedding during which I, as the stepfather, wondered anew, even after almost eight years, how things would go. How should I be supportive of my stepchildren without assuming an inappropriate role? In the middle of the reception, my youngest stepdaughter came over to me, threw her arms around me, and said some deeply personal things about how she felt about me. It is hard to describe how moved I was. For us to have reached that special moment, a lot of time had elapsed and a lot of growing up together had taken place. Believe me, it was worth the wait. Believe me, when I tell you it probably couldn't have happened any sooner than it did!

MONEY, POWER, AND CONTROL

Say you don't need no diamond rings and
I'll be satisfied
Tell me that you want the kind of things
that money just can't buy
I don't care too much for money
Money can't buy me love

—JOHN LENNON AND PAUL MCCARTNEY
("Can't Buy Me Love")

*M*oney begets power and power begets control. That sounds Biblical and it is just as ancient, for the interconnections between these three has intrigued, influenced, and confused human beings for centuries. Years ago I participated in an exercise at a racial attitudes conference that tried to show their interconnection and how we behaved with *and* without money. Those "without" behaved in a very different way from those "with" and what was more fascinating was to see the attitudes of those whose real life roles were reversed.

Having money may bring problems with it but nothing like not having the cash to live on! These pressures can warp a marriage quicker than anything I know because scrabbling for the basics requires enormous energy, leaving little time for anything else. Also the emotional drain of living hand-to-mouth can be devastating. There are no easy answers to this increasingly frequent dilemma.

Money is so central to our daily economic and emotional well-being that partners, especially marriage partners, must understand its dynamics and how the other feels about money. Money, or the lack of it, can do terrible things to people, if it is not understood as a means, not an end, as the gas and not the engine, as something to use and not be used by! Greed has been around a long time and, if acquisitiveness seduces us early, it is hard to shake later on.

One cardinal rule to remember: Money is necessary, *but* it is *not* the key to happiness or a good marriage or a full life. Money buys goods, not goodness. Money provides what we need to exist, but beyond that, it is like a picture on a wall or a boat—nice but not essential. If you can put human needs first and human wants eighth or ninth, you will be better off emotionally and economically.

WHOSE MONEY IS IT?

Some partners bring unearned money to a marriage. Inheritance or savings are nice, but you must decide *before* the marriage, if at all possible, how this money will be used and by whom. Romantics and opportunists will say "it's our money," but it is not! It is either your money or your spouse's money, and that has to be acknowledged up front. Only then will you both be able to talk about its use. Couples work out various arrangements. Some use her money for extraordinary expenses, such as a special dress or a vacation; some use his money to start a savings account for the children or for a down payment on a house. These are decisions both can be happy with, but "the owner's right" must be acknowledged. If it isn't, these outside dollars can become a wedge to leverage one's own will, or worse, a weapon to embarrass or control the other partner.

One proven way to put an entirely new cast on unearned money is to give some of it away each year. It dilutes the guilt and enhances your own sense of the "better" use of money. The decision to do this is made by "the owner," but *where* to give it might be a joint decision. Starting with what you give to others, rather than what you spend on yourself somehow changes your priorities and thus lessens the problems unearned money can cause.

PARTNERS IN EARNING

Earned money creates similar dilemmas, but here, *who* earns it carries less weight, for both partners must decide on how it is to be used. What complicates a marriage are the feelings about how much is earned and by whom! A high female earner or the "nonworking" wife of a male earner both feel they have rights—different perhaps, but still rights. I would wager that the husband of either one might feel differently; in the first case, a little uneasy and jealous; in the second, a little bit more in charge, since he is "the provider."

"Women's work is never done" is the old adage. It is true, even today, in our more emancipated society in which both partners are often employed. There are few husbands who could afford to pay a person to do as much as a wife and mother does in the course of a normal day, often *after* a day at the office! That's if they could find such a person in the first place. Women are earners in the finest sense of that word and need to be acknowledged as such. Men are the traditional providers and they too need a pat and a hug. Both work hard. Their hours can be unreal, but sometimes get that way because of a perception, real or unreal, of what is expected of them at home. Both earners should sit down and figure out what they need financially and emotionally!

PARTNERS IN SPENDING

Some jokester wrote, "Why is there so much month left at the end of the money?" Regardless of how much money is coming in, there is inevitably a shortfall before or at the end of the month.

Partners should set priorities, budget, keep track of where daily money is being spent, and together decide what major expenditures are to be made and how they will be financed. You do this in business. Why should home economics be any different? Reasonable minds can differ and it takes "reasonable minds" to quietly and objectively talk about how money should be spent.

I know one couple who had a large income, but who were always broke. They decided to keep a daily record of *every* penny spent, from newspapers to taxis to lunches to necessities. It sounds overly tedious, but it worked. They were able to identify and agree on those areas in which they were spending too much money, often without realizing it.

Some couples review their checkbook together at the end of the month to see how much they spend and why. Others make a joint decision to lock up their charge cards until they get back on track. Whatever you do, it is important that you feel like a willing participant, not an angry bystander, when it comes to the spending of money. Money is dynamite. Treat it with extreme care!

PARTNERS IN SAVING

It is tough to save money these days, but it is a worthy goal! Major expected and unexpected expenditures come up with amazing regularity, and it helps to have a little extra stashed away to help ease the blow. Putting money aside, even if it is only a few dollars every month, provides a cushion and, more important, peace of mind. Feeling strapped is bad enough, but feeling totally destitute is literally frightening.

By the way, there is no way you can save enough now to

educate your children later. You will somehow find the money or the loans or the scholarships for college when that time comes. Too many people fall into the trap of depriving themselves now for the sake of future education. Don't fall into this trap. Give to yourself, your spouse, and your children now. The solutions for the future will come when they are needed.

PARTNERS IN GIVING

Giving money is the last money issue to be discussed, but it should really be the first in our considerations as marriage partners. Whatever your resources, giving part of it away every year is a healthy, helpful, and wonderful gesture. It keeps money in proper perspective. It keeps us aware that money is evidence of what we do for a living and not what living is all about. It keeps our integrity and our sense of responsibility for our "neighbors" intact. It keeps us from spending willfully on ourselves and being blind to our obligation to do for others what has been done for us.

The happiest people I know are those who give away more than they probably should, but who believe that giving is living in the deepest sense of that word. If we, as marriage partners, budget a percentage of our expected income to give away, at the beginning of the year, then we can enjoy the process of choosing, over the next eleven months, who gets what and for what purpose. If we wait to see what's left over at the end of the year, the money is all gone, and little, if any, will go beyond our own walls.

THE BALANCE OF POWER AND CONTROL

Power and control go together, for people who have or assume power inevitably want to take control. Money is a means to power and its use or misuse can exercise enormous control over those who don't have it. To be successful a marriage must maintain a balance of power and control. Their use or misuse within a marriage partnership can literally make or break it.

We all have power. We all want to be in control. If we as individuals and as partners can admit that, we are on our way to understanding and managing our proclivity to grab the first and abuse the second.

Power is given and taken. Men still have more visible power because of history, custom, physical strength, and traditional roles. Women still have less power, because of societal customs and laws, but they usually exercise better what they do have! Long before the current, long overdue efforts to equalize roles and responsibilities and compensation, women used their considerable power to stop armies (Deborah killing Jael), stop wars (the story of Lysistrata), stop injustice (Esther unmasking Haman), run countries (Elizabeth I, Catherine the Great, Golda Meir, Margaret Thatcher), and force necessary changes to be made (ERA, NOW, MADD) just to mention a few.

Let me tell you about a very graphic exercise used by a therapist in New York. She has the wife kneel with her hands on the floor like a prisoner. Then she has the husband stand next to her, with one foot on her back and his arms crossed like the mighty conqueror. Then she asks "who has the power?" The answer is, the wife does! All she needs to do is move just a little, one way or the other, and the man will topple to the ground. This dramatically demonstrates that what seems like power often isn't, and that each one of us has more power than we think we do.

FEELING THREATENED

Society and law notwithstanding, the equalization of power is now a more open forum and a powerful movement throughout the world. The real changes will have taken place, however, when marriage partners can talk out and work out their control needs and actions, so that each partner feels he or she shares control of their joint enterprise. That means each has to give up manipulation and attempting to manage the other.

Business partners have to share the management of their firm or neither one will be on top of things. Business partners are both familiar with the books. They share tasks and work together to make a success out of their endeavor. Business partners both cede and assume power, ask and give advice, and put the business ahead of their own hangups. Why should marriage partnerships be any different?

There is a key word here and I think it applies to men and women alike. *Threatened.* When we feel threatened, either as a husband who is not secure enough to include his wife in his confusions and conflicts, or as a wife who is not secure enough to speak up and stand up for her rights, we figuratively "head for the hills." To use more regal terms, we either hide behind our crown or we abdicate. Neither path is the road to a successful, profitable, egalitarian partnership.

For a couple to deal openly and wisely with the control and power question, they need to communicate. The following two exercises are designed to help:

EXERCISE 10
Make Agreements

1. Make a verbal contract that, like business partners, you each "own" or control half the marriage and, therefore, each have fifty percent of the voting power!

    This reverses and puts the control question first! If each of you can really feel *and* experience a sense of control over the direction and operation of your common enterprise, who has power over which segment of the whole can usually be negotiated.

2. Prepare a written agreement (even if in outline form) listing the major and minor function/decision areas and pinpointing who is in charge of what.

    In some cases it may have to be a joint decision; in others, one partner's expertise may be a factor. In any case, assign responsibility and authority and follow this game plan for at least three months. This may sound too pragmatic or even too contrived. It may be both, but try it anyway. By doing this exercise in good faith, for the right reasons, you may find a better way to deal with your partnership, your marriage partner, and your own "threatened" self.

Here are some examples of step number two in action:

Function/Decision Areas	Responsibility and Authority	Notes
Pay bills/keeping the checkbook	Hers	Both review expenditures every three months.
Buying a car	Shared (or no car!)	He does the research.
Investments	His	Her input encouraged.
Cooking	Hers	
Cleaning up	His	
Vacation	Shared	She does the research.
Budget	Hers	His input expected.
Grocery shopping	Hers	His input not expected!
Lawn care	His	She tends the flowers.

These may sound commonplace, but it is within the mundane events of everyday life that power and control issues always come up. This list is just a beginning. It deals with simpler issues, but this is where to begin.

LETTING GO OF POWER

Power and control are the subject, not the object, of a partnership. If you love and respect and trust your partner's intentions and judgments, you can give them a chance to be your partner in every sense of that word.

To let someone else drive you in a car or prescribe medicine or sell you a house is automatically giving up control. You cede to them a degree of power over you. If it is that simple in those examples why can't you do the same thing at home? Ceding power because you freely choose to do so is *not* losing it. It increases it! It takes it out of the context of me, me, me and turns it upside down into we, we, we. Everyone feels better, more gets done, and our partnership can function, improve, deepen, and grow!

CAREERS, VOCATIONS, AND DREAMS

Those who dream by day are cognizant of many things which escape those who dream only by night.

—EDGAR ALLAN POE,
("Elenora")

*M*y career is being an author, businessman, mission priest, and community activist. My vocation is to reach out to people through my words and actions—particularly those who are stuck or who have been dealt a lousy hand. My dream is to expand my horizons and even climb some new mountains as the years go on. But I am fifty-seven years old and have traveled a far distance *and* have gone through the very thinking process I suggest to you.

What "we do" becomes so much a part of what "we are" that our careers and vocations are central to our emotional well-being. I think it is fair to say that, if we are miserable at work, we will be miserable at home. That is why what you do professionally should be examined at regular intervals during the course of your working life. Just because you started out as a stockbroker or house painter or teacher does not *mean* that you have to spend the rest of your life as a stockbroker or house painter or teacher.

A vocation is what energizes us. A career is how we live it out. Vocations can change. Multiple careers are possible. In fact, individuals and partners who have the courage to look at other options and to envision how the quality of their lives would be affected enrich their relationships. As partners with a common goal, a full and satisfying and secure life, they can afford to at least be honest about what they now do and what more they might like to do!

TAPPING UNTAPPED RESOURCES

In my role as a counselor I have heard successful investment bankers talk about going into the ministry, doctors wondering why they ever chose medicine in the first place, businessmen considering farming, housewives discussing becoming therapists—the list goes on and on. I have also heard many men and women talk excitedly about what they are doing and how much fulfillment and enjoyment they receive from it. My point is that it is okay to be satisfied and it is okay to be looking around. The trick is to know when either "satisfaction" or "dissatisfaction" is being used as an escape from reality.

When we think of vocations we think of what moves and

motivates us on a deeper level. Careers are the way we act out our instincts and our particular interests. Vocations can often be unfulfilled because of circumstances beyond our control. Careers can often be unsatisfying for the same reasons. The ideal is to match them as closely as possible, recognizing the realities and pressures of daily living.

Maybe my own experience, my journey, will help make this clearer. As a young man I was intrigued by business. I came from a family whose involvement in business was long and successful. I got a Master's in business administration, then spent fifteen years as a businessman. I enjoyed it, I was challenged by it, I learned and accomplished a lot. But I began to have a nagging (not entirely new, for it had haunted me before) that I wanted to study for the ministry. I put off any decision for a year in order to test my feelings and to make certain I wasn't falling into the trap of believing that "the grass was greener on the other side of the fence." During this year my business career was actually at its peak, but the nagging grew. After a lot of thought and conversation and prayer I decided to go to seminary. It was hard work, but it was wonderful, and when I was finally ordained a priest I felt I had truly come home.

For twenty years thereafter I was a parish priest. I loved it and I think I was good at it. I carried no regrets about leaving business and, in fact, was able to use my prior experience in my preaching, my pastoral work, and my community involvement. After two very different, but very challenging and satisfying rectorships, I began to dream about a third career. My vocation as a priest was secure, but I wondered if I couldn't exercise it in less traditional ways.

I had always wanted to write. I had a deep interest in clergy who were "stuck" and needed pragmatic counseling to help them either get reorganized in what they were doing or take a look at other possible options. I had an interest in parish consultation and I felt deeply that I wanted to "give back something" by being more available for community service. I left the parish ministry and became a supply priest (a circuit rider!), writer, consultant, and community activist. My new career—*same vocation*—has worked out extraordinarily well and, as someone said about his own experience, "It has been the crown of my ministry." I did have the advantage of some economic independence, which I realize made my journey far less anxious. Nevertheless, I still had to deal with my personal, professional, and emotional hopes, fears, and realities as I embarked on each of these new careers. As someone used to say, "I am happy as a grig," and my own life and close relationships reflect that!

I am not recommending what I did as a model for anyone else. What I'm trying to point out is that within each of you are untapped resources, untapped ideas, untapped possibilities that could make a difference in the quality of your individual lives and your marriage partnership.

BRANCHING OUT, TAKING CHANCES

A periodic personal inventory helps a lot. How to do this depends on personal preference. Some people keep it to themselves. More, I hope, share such explorations with their partners; and even more check it out with somebody who is more objective. There are four basic questions later in this chapter that can be asked and dealt with at almost any stage in your life. They are designed to help you take a personal inventory of your feelings about your work. The only requirement is that you be willing to look at change—change as an opportunity to go beyond or at least dream beyond the frame of life that you now see yourself encased in. Try the next exercise, taken from an old parlor game.

EXERCISE 11
Connect the Dots

1. Try to connect nine dots with four straight lines without lifting your pencil from the paper.

    •   •   •

    •   •   •

    •   •   •

2. You try and try again and say it is impossible. But look below. If you have to stay strictly within that boxlike structure; it *is* impossible. But if you are willing to go beyond the lines, branch out, to do the unusual and take a chance, the puzzle *can* be solved!

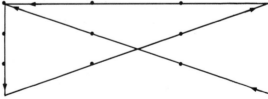

You changed the dimensions. You redefined the problem.

You were willing to go beyond what you thought were your limitations. Bravo! You have begun to think in new and creative and expanded ways *and* you still played within the rules.

Reflection isn't a luxury. It's a necessity. You owe it to yourself and your partner to take your own pulse, check your perceptions and performance, those deeper feelings and thoughts that keep surfacing. Find a comfortable and private place. Set aside an hour. Take a pencil and legal pad. Focus on YOU: what you want, what you want to do, what you can do, and what you will do! Write. Brainstorm. Be free enough to dream and take yourself seriously—seriously enough to realize that it is your life, your future, and your inner peace that is at stake. If that is in perspective, your marriage will be strengthened also.

THE FOUR QUESTIONS

EXERCISE 12
The First Question

Ask yourself, "What do I want?" What are your deepest needs and wants? Some answers might be more joy in life, financial security, a different job; others might be more (or less) responsibility in your present job, a happier marriage, a community you feel more comfortable and welcome in, a deeper faith in God, to take better care of your mind and body, to relax and enjoy a bit more, a better sex life, to own a Mercedes, to read more, to be more creative and useful in what you do every day, to be a nicer person, to worry less about everything—and these might just be openers.

By focusing solely on what you want and being honest about wanting it, you get a better picture of what makes you what you are and hope to be. That looks so easy but it is very tough to do, for we all tend to let the answer to this first question overlap into the questions that follow.

Think hard and write down everything and anything that comes to mind. Acknowledge what is deep in your heart. *Take time, and write it down.* No one will see the list or pass judgment on it, so you can be totally truthful, willful, and free.

EXERCISE 13
The Second Question

Ask yourself, "What do I want to do?"

This is a different question because of the last two words, but again, reality should not govern what you say. You might list, for instance, move to Florida, go back to law school, leave business and teach, be a congressman, become president of a Fortune 500 company, spend more time with my wife, get into the country club, write poetry, run a restaurant, make a lot of money, reorganize my present job, control my workaholism, give up cigars—and more and more specific things that you would like to do for a variety of reasons. This is a list that begins to focus on what you "might" like to actually do with your life if you had your "druthers"!

Unless you are willing to admit these, out loud to yourself, you may never uncover that potential key to change that might literally change your life. Sometimes what seems at first to be a crazy notion or an outlandish thought will, on further perusal, turn into the germ of an idea that might even be workable! By spreading these out on paper, without censorship, you may be able to see a range and a connection that is simply impossible to compute in your head.

EXERCISE 14
The Third Question

Ask yourself, "What can I do"?

Here we get into reality and here we cannot afford to take flights of fancy. For instance, I might put down "I can run a business and be a parish priest," both of which I know I can do. But for me to put down that I could teach French literature at the Sorbonne would be totally unreal for I know very little about literature and can hardly speak a word of French.

Your list might contain:

1. Things you know you can do because you actually have done them.
2. Things you can do that you haven't even considered because of elapsed time or past experiences. Sometimes out of the past come interesting options that just might work now.

3. New combinations out of your experiences and your dreams. For example, I could be a community organizer, although I've never formally done that, but I have helped organize "emergency alliances" in my role as a parish clergyman. I have written sermons for years, so for me to become an "author" could be looked on as simply stringing together a series of sermons. You see how these connections are made and how this can fall into place? Be realistic and very sure of your boundaries and your competence. This list will be shorter than the other two, but that is how it should be for it becomes the baseline for the next question and your eventual determinations.

EXERCISE 15
The Question: Putting It All Together

Ask yourself, "What will I do?"

How many times, in the middle of the night, have we laid awake dreaming, considering, measuring, filtering, even planning a new vocation or a change in career or different job. What you do is such an integral part of who you are that these nocturnal perusings are one way of you dealing with the internal and sometimes external pressure on you to do something different.

1. Look back over the answers to Exercise 13. Underline those that really turn you on. Pencil through those that seem fanciful.
2. Look at the answers to Exercise 14. Underline those that

you really enjoy doing or did enjoy doing. Pencil through those that turn you off, including your present occupation, if it falls into that category.

3. Combine the lists and see what you've got. I bet you'll find new combinations, new possibilities, or maybe even a new sense of purpose in what you are already doing? In any case, come up with a final list in order of priority after blending in the answers to Exercise 12. Now you can more accurately reflect what you might like to do next with your acumen, your time, your expertise, your experience and your lives.

DREAMING

You say this sounds like dreaming. It is! That is just the point. We all need to dream, look over the wall, expand our horizons, go outside the square, "the nine dots" that we think contain and confine us. Dream outrageous dreams and then take from them the energy and the ideas that suit your particular situation and purposes. You can dream alone *but* remember this:

1. Partners who dream together expand each other. One's dreams feed another's.
2. Partners who love and respect and trust each other can moderate or redirect or encourage the train and direction of thought.

3. Partners have to live with whatever dreams become reality, so it is essential to be in on them from the start.

I think dreaming is a way to both clear and focus our minds. Like a free-fall parachute jump, there are no restraints until the ripcord is pulled, and not unlike that experience, we are the ones who literally have to pull ourselves back into reality. But it is the experience itself that is so incredible. Dreaming helps us cope with our fantasies, without trying to actually act them out. Dreaming raises our sights and allows our minds to explore angles and corners never before explored. Even daydreaming is healthy, natural, and not injurious to our health. In fact, quite the opposite. It unlocks a part of our mind that can entertain, enhance, excite, and encourage us to be more and better than we thought we were.

Edgar Allan Poe was right. "Those who dream by day are cognizant of many things which escape those who dream only by night." We might remember that, as we look in the mirror of our discontent and try to see behind and beyond the familiar images—the jobs we've been doing for twenty years, the ruts we feel we are in, the humdrum patterns of life we can't seem to do anything about. We might also remember that, in the last analysis, you and I *are* in charge of who we are and what we do. We may not be able to change things very drastically or dramatically, but we can affect change in our lives one way or another. Dreaming may well get us going, but it is our willingness to look at changing patterns, habits, locations, jobs, or even vocations that will keep us alive, alert, and healthy. Partnerships and individual partners thrive on this kind of stimuli. Partnerships are always looking for "infusion of new capital and talent" and that is just what comes when we turn on the lights inside our minds.

Finally let me say that dreaming is something more, far more—it is a searching out, the searching of our souls, the searching into our deepest and most private selves. Why is it so important to a marriage, a partnership of love? It is important because our better instincts are often buried beneath what is and what has been. They need surfacing and a chance to breathe. It is important because those rare moments when we as couples dig deep and talk deep are when we are closest. It is important because when we dream, we are nearer God and as William Shakespeare reminds us in *Henry V* (Act V): "God, the best maker of all marriages, Combine your hearts in one."

PLAY

Holidays should be like this,
Free from overemphasis
Time for soul to stretch and spit
Before the world comes back on it.

—LOUIS MACNEICE
(Epilogue for Witt. Auden)

"*P*lay" comes at the end of this book because that is usually where we put it on our list of things to do! That's not right, but perhaps this will help us realize our error and convince us that play—rest, recreation, vacations—should be assigned a much higher priority. They are *essential* to our mental, physical, and marital health.

THE REAL WORLD

People frequently come back from vacation and remark "That was fun, but now I'm back in the real world." I always want to shout, "No. You are wrong. You probably have been a far nicer person, partner, and parent during this vacation than you have been during the past eleven and a half months!" Vacation time—that is the real world! You focus more attention on other people; you allow yourself to have fun; you give your body rest and pleasure and exercise; you let your mind wander off into so-called nonproductive arenas such as reading or self-contemplation or daydreaming; you also re-center and rejuvenate your partnership in healthy and helpful ways.

It is precisely this free spiritedness-this play—that you need to incorporate more into your everyday life—the real world we refer to. The real you and the real me need regular opportunities to re-engage with our better selves. We need time off to relax, regroup, refresh, and renew our marriages.

RECREATION IS RE-CREATION

Vacations are usually given to you by someone else, but you must learn to give vacations to yourself. Individuals need individual play time. The old saying, "All work and no play makes Jack a dull boy" did not come out of thin air.

Set aside time each day to do exactly what you want, from jogging to meditating to reading to sitting on your porch puffing an occasional cigar. No one will tell you to do this, so you have to take yourself and your family seriously enough to carve out this private play time every day. Why is it so important to play by yourself? I think we not only crave a change from all the confusions of life, but we also require some solitary time. I realize this is often easier said than done, but in terms of long-range health, it could be the best fifteen- to thirty-minute daily investment you could make.

TAKE A DAY OFF ALONE

Every once in a while, take a "mental health" day off and just play by yourself. What should you do? Perhaps it has been so long since you've had some time off, you don't even know what you want to do. Experiment! Literally "let it happen." I tried this once when my family was away on a Saturday. I woke up hours before I had planned to, but it was a beautiful day and I fancied a long walk. We lived at the time in New York City. I got up and walked from Ninety-third Street to Twenty-third Street. Few people were about and it was a beautiful morning. I walked and looked in windows and looked at people. I had breakfast in a coffee shop and enjoyed foods I normally didn't eat at home. I walked up Madison Avenue, as I'd walked down fifth, and "spent a million dollars with my eyes." I bought a cigar, sat in the park opposite the Plaza Hotel, and spent an hour just looking as the world passed me by! I won't bore you with the details of what else I did that day. The point is I let it happen—evolve—and I had a wonderful day. I felt like a rejuvenated person when I finally fell into bed that night. It opened my eyes to the fact that taking such a day for myself was not just healthy, but a lot of fun, as well.

I like to jog a couple of miles each day. It is fun for me. It keeps my heart pumping. It also gives me time to be alone with God and myself and nature for about twenty minutes. I know people who write poetry, take naps, build models, just sit and look at the sea or into the fire. What you do is not as important as the fact that you do something recreational on a regular basis that diverts and stretches your mind and your body too. *Recreation is literally re-creation* and this is what healthy people do to stay that way above and below the neck!

TIME OUT FOR PARENTS

Being parents can be tough on a relationship. One factor to overcome is the guilt and pressures that keep telling you "we can't leave the children." You not only can, you must! Time spent together, away from the children, can be the most important and constructive time for you and will strengthen you in your roles as parents. You will be better off for it, and the kids will grow up with a much better example. Remember, they want time away from you, too!

Partners need to plan private time and privacy, *including* locked bedrooms after lights out. Children do not need open access to your bedroom. They can knock, just like we knock on theirs when they get older. The secondary gain is to teach your children about privacy. The primary gain is to assure yourselves of some private time together so that you can make love or do whatever you darn well please.

Normal days are crammed full of business and busy activities, yet each day still has some time left over for a few minutes alone together before getting up, sharing something from the newspaper at breakfast, a mid-morning call, an occasional lunch, "adult" time before dinner, a late-hour date for talking, laughing, loving. This may sound romantic and unreal, but each of you, *if you want to*, can carve out of each day some private fun time. If you don't, you run the risk of beginning to lead separate lives—first at home, then outside—and this spells disaster for your partnership.

Trips are also important, and marriage partners should take at least one pure pleasure trip each year away from business and away from the children. "I'll do just a couple of days' work," or "The kids would love to see this" are often-heard excuses that mess up priorities and mess up vacations. You cannot have it both ways. Believe me, when couples can sneak away alone for some R & R, their partnerships improve, their personalities improve, their sex lives improve, their balances improve, and their energy and enthusiasm for their joint enterprise improve! I've seen couples bask on a Caribbean beach for a week and return with a whole new outlook on life and on each other. It is truly amazing what can happen when couples realize it is vital to plan regular recreational times and annual vacations for play.

ENJOYING EACH OTHER

Another aspect of having fun is simply enjoying each other—really liking and engaging each other "at work" and at play. Sometimes this happens in the simplest of ways: walking hand in hand, sharing an observation, feeling and saying something silly, laughing at an old joke, humming an old tune. You can spot people who like each other by the way they connect. You can feel their joy and the humor they radiate. They laugh with their eyes, as well as with their mouths. They see the ridiculous, as well as the serious, in themselves. In other words, they are able to have fun—not as a separate segment of life, but as an integral part of their daily living. There is no formula for this—only what we learn from those who have that innate ability to love each other and life enough to obsess a little less and relax a little more and to laugh at themselves. "Playing" is one way to set the stage for this to happen.

We all get trapped in our own fantasies about how indispensable we are *and* we forget that we are the ones who keep our appointment books! What is your reaction to these do's and don'ts?

- Don't assume that your company, your career, or your work can't get along without you. They can! You're the one who can't get along without them, or think you can't.
- Do plan ahead for "couple time" and family time, week by week. It just doesn't happen by itself. It is too easy to let other demands crowd them out.
- Don't take yourself too seriously for too long. Laughter can help you take off your mask and be a more joyful human being.
- Do not substitute office fun for fun at home. You have to get away from what you do for a living to be able to relax enough to taste the true enjoyments of life.
- Do get away. Vacation, travel, do something totally nonpro-

ductive at least twice a year and at least once alone with your spouse.

- Don't rely on artificial means such as alcohol or drugs to relax and loosen up. Getting crocked or high changes the balances and can lead to words and actions that shatter the very peace and calm and fun you're seeking.

It is hard to follow this advice. I know, for I don't always practice what I preach. It has taken me years to be able to read a book purely for pleasure without wondering if I should be reading a theological tome instead. It is hard for me, even now, to sit and do nothing for a week, even though I feel one hundred percent better for the experience. Fun doesn't come easy for "puritans," but nowhere in the Bible, or anywhere else for that matter, is there a prohibition against having a good time. If you make it a high priority, you needn't fear being consumed by it. If you make it a low priority, you will be forever putting it off.

Relax and enjoy. They are two of the hardest words to internalize but if you can, your life will never be the same again. It will be infinitely better! You will be a better person. Your children and families will have a much better time! In fact, this book may end up being a better book, if I stop writing about "play" and actually go ahead and have some fun myself—*right now!*

CRUCIAL QUESTIONS

The following exercises are three quite separate questionnaires that my wife and I have used in our counseling work. PLEASE BE VERY CAREFUL HOW YOU USE THEM. They are better used under the supervision of a counselor/therapist or minister, for "a third party" can defuse and redirect potentially explosive answers!

Exercise 16 is what I used with couples prior to their actual marriages. It can also be used for couples who have run into rough water. The questions are basic to any solid partnership. They need to be dealt with individually and privately before being shared with "the partner." I used them in our joint conferences and only then allowed each member of the couple to see how the other had answered. Couples who took the time to answer these questions thoughtfully and honestly found this experience broadening and helpful in their understanding of what their partner was actually feeling!

EXERCISE 16
Questions You Should Ask

Take a moment to answer the following questions. Write them down. Be specific. Be honest.

1. What are your personal priorities?
2. What are your expectations from this marriage?
   Emotional
   Sexual
   Spiritual
   Family
   Economic

3. What is your overall life plan?
4. What do you like most about yourself?
5. What would you like to see changed in your own behavior?
6. What do you like most about your partner?
7. What would you like to see changed in his/her behavior?
8. What do you as a couple have to offer?
9. How would you describe your sexual relationship and are you satisfied with it?
10. How do you deal with feelings, such as anger, joy, sadness?
11. How do you and your partner resolve conflict?
12. How do you feel about touching, hugging and holding?
13. What role does God/faith play in your life?
14. How do you feel about seeking therapeutic help?
15. How would you describe an "intimate" relationship?
16. Do you think this relationship could fail, and if so, why?
17. What role does money play in your life?
18. How do you feel about your family of origin, in-laws, and children (if any)?
19. What is fun for you?
20. How do you and your partner play?
21. Are you or your partner addicted to anything? (Liquor? Tobacco? TV? Sports? Work?) Be honest.
22. Are there any secrets that you cannot share with your partner?
23. How would you feel about your partner knowing your answers to these questions?
24. If something happened to your partner's health or job or reputation, how could you cope?
25. Why do you (or did you) want to get married?

26. Other than for love, why do you (or did you) want to marry this particular person?
27. Are there specific things worrying you about this relationship/marriage?

EXERCISE 17
Questions You Should Be Asked By Someone Else

Exercise 17 is for a troubled person or couple to help them take a long and hard look at what has gone wrong and why. There are tough questions here that focus on what has happened, what could happen, and what can happen to the partners involved. Particularly here, these should be thought out and written out alone and used by the individual *and* the counselor to help sort out the mess he or she is in *and* the mess he/she might be getting in if no changes are made. Couples should not share these. It just doesn't help!

1. Why do you seek help?
2. Why do you seek help now?
3. Have you tried to solve this problem and how?
4. List ten problems that affect your relationship with your spouse.
5. List five problems that you think your spouse has with this marriage.
6. In your relationship, who has the final word and why?
7. What outside influences affect this marriage? (Job, friends, family, children, ex-mate, liquor, sports, etc.)

Positive Influences	Negative Influences

8. How well do you and your spouse communicate?
   Overall_____Emotionally_____Intellectually_____
   Professionally_____Spiritually_____Sexually_____
   Rating: 10 (Great) to 1 (Lousy)
9. When you fight, what happens?
10. How would you define an ideal marriage? (Write at least one hundred words.)
11. Please describe in chart/outline form your *and* your spouse's genealogy and background, going back to grandparents and forward to any children or grandchildren you may have and including all your siblings. Rate next to each name which ones you like a lot (10) to not at all (1). Note if anyone shown has had any serious problems (divorce, alcoholism, sickness, etc.).

EXERCISE 18

Exercise 18 is a perception chart to measure how individuals perceive the various aspects of their relationship. It has to do with how WE perceive, *not* how we think our partners might like us to perceive. There are no right or wrong answers. Answers can change overnight. The point of this exercise is to find out where there are wide differences in how two people look at the same thing. For example, if under Romantic Attraction you circle a 2 and I circle a 10, we've got a problem! This tool can help a therapist or clergyperson delve into these differences and try to bridge them. Partners need to perceive the facets of their relationship in some concert (within a 2 to 4 point spread) and if not, they need to know why! DO NOT SHOW YOUR CHART TO YOUR SPOUSE. Let the third party be the interpreter and the buffer.

On the graph on the next page, please rate how *you* see the relationship with your partner *as of today*. Dot each choice and then connect them. SCALE: 1 is POOR—5 is AVERAGE—10 is GOOD.

	1	2	3	4	5	6	7	8	9	10
Romantic Attraction										
Emotional Stability										
Sexual Relationship										
Communicating										
Financial Understanding										
Expressing Anger										
Spiritual Awareness										
Sharing Feelings										
Fighting with Each Other										
Accepting "Differences"										
Caring for Each Other										
Sharing with Each Other										
Forgiving Each Other										
Making Major Decisions										
Making Minor Decisions										
Jealousy										
Having Fun Together										
Dealing With Families										
Dealing with Children										
Dealing with Friends										

1   2   3   4   5   6   7   8   9   10

INDEX